Prayer in the Writings of Jean-Jacques Rousseau

PETER LANG
New York • Washington, D.C./Baltimore • Bern
Frankfurt am Main • Berlin • Brussels • Vienna • Oxford

Charles A. Spirn

Prayer in the Writings
of Jean-Jacques Rousseau

PETER LANG
New York • Washington, D.C./Baltimore • Bern
Frankfurt am Main • Berlin • Brussels • Vienna • Oxford

Library of Congress Cataloging-in-Publication Data

Spirn, Charles A.
Prayer in the writings of Jean-Jacques Rousseau / Charles A. Spirn.
p. cm.
Includes bibliographical references.
1. Rousseau, Jean-Jacques, 1712–1778. 2. Prayer. I. Title.
B2138.R4S65   248.3'2092–dc22   2007046364
ISBN 978-1-4331-0138-0

Bibliographic information published by **Die Deutsche Bibliothek**.
Die Deutsche Bibliothek lists this publication in the "Deutsche
Nationalbibliografie"; detailed bibliographic data is available
on the Internet at http://dnb.ddb.de/.

B
2138
.R4
S65
2008

The paper in this book meets the guidelines for permanence and durability
of the Committee on Production Guidelines for Book Longevity
of the Council of Library Resources.

© 2008 Peter Lang Publishing, Inc., New York
29 Broadway, 18th floor, New York, NY 10006
www.peterlang.com

Printed in the United States of America

Dedicated to
Professor Otis E. Fellows
wise and inspiring scholar, teacher, author and faculty advisor
who personifies the noblest ideals
of true humanism,
with a prayer
for good health, long life and continued achievement

Table of Contents

Acknowledgments

I would like to express my profound gratitude to Professor Otis E. Fellows who stood at the inception of the theme of this dissertation during my course at Columbia University on eighteenth-century French literature and who, by his constant and steady encouragement and support, saw it come to fruition. He never limited himself just to the formal role of faculty sponsor and advisor but guided and inspired me to go on and pursue my research work and, at moments of discouragement, knew the right words to prompt me to persevere. He supported me both with his scholarly advice and his personal interest and gave generously of his time. I dedicate this study to my scholarly and beloved mentor as an expression of my deeply-felt appreciation, admiration, and affection.

My thanks also go to Professor Jean Sareil, the second reader, for his careful study of the dissertation and his judicious comments and corrections, which I value very highly.

Special acknowledgment is due to my dear and devoted wife, Dr. Regina Spirn, whose inspiration and dependable presence and advice helped considerably in my moving ahead in this task. Though herself a scientist, she utilized her flair for language and discernment in literature to read the manuscript with much care and patience and offered many constructive suggestions. Our dear children, Beth and Neil, too, became involved in their contagious rejoicing over the progress of this work, in addition to their unfailing love and sense of pride.

The expertise of Mrs. W. T. H. Jackson in both English and French, her willingness to work from a handwritten manuscript and her detailed knowledge of all aspects of typing a dissertation proved to be of crucial importance in getting it presented in time. She has been a godsend indeed. I am pleased to express here my profound appreciation for her help as well as for the advice of her learned husband, Professor Jackson.

Of particular assistance enabling me to work home was my dear friend, Dr. Benjamin Klebaner, professor of economics and former assistant dean of the City College of New York, for making available to me the writings of Rousseau and other authors and critics. My sincere thanks also go to Mr. Charles Wirz, secretary of the "Société Jean-Jacques Rousseau" in Geneva, Switzerland, for his kind and prompt response to my inquiry about the location of a specific passage in the voluminous correspondence of Rousseau.

To the scholarly and friendly faculty members of the Graduate Department of French and Romance Philology of Columbia University goes my gratitude for the instruction I received from them and the knowledge I gained. It all came to fruition in the writing of this dissertation.

CHAPTER I

Introduction

The French eighteenth century—the Age of Enlightenment and of Reason—has been looked upon as the age of skepticism, of materialistic humanism, of irreligiosity and, to be sure, of deism. If such a view is valid, we might least expect the presence of prayers in the writings of the literary standard-bearers of the age. For rationalism as a method of finding truth was to be found in all disciplines. After having been the sovereign arbiter in a few restricted fields, reasoning suddenly became the leading arbiter in all domains, even that of religious faith. Bossuet's foreboding proved justified; he had foreseen powerful forces rising against the Church in the name of Cartesian philosophy. In the name of freedom, he believed, they would brush aside tradition and boldly advance any thought they wished. It was manifestly the principle of methodical doubt in Descartes' philosophy that the prelate thought to be of greatest concern. The century has with good reason been looked upon as an age of skepticism, of reversal of authority, of materialistic humanism, of irreligiosity and, to be sure, of deism. Particularly in the second half of the century, literature became audacious, militant, committed. Many reasons have been suggested, as Professor Norman L. Torrey tells us, "for the comparatively sudden and almost simultaneous entry into the field of deistic criticism of Voltaire, Rousseau and d'Holbach." Torrey adds: "A change in public opinion and a weakening of authority had taken place which removed fear of persecution and manifested itself in the expulsion of the Jesuits."[1] Everything, then, was put in question in religion and politics which were attacked so as to be reconstructed on different foundations.

---

[1] Norman L. Torrey, *Voltaire and the English Deists* (Hamden, Conn.: Archon Books, 1967), p. 8.

During this century, we might least expect the presence of prayers in the writings of its literary standard-bearers. Yet, during that age, as during others—in some ways even more so—individuals and groups felt the need to commune with a force greater than they. For if the eighteenth century in France had its traditional groups, its organized religions that followed their forbears in communing with the Supreme Being, it was also an age of disquietude, of a new awareness of the mechanical nature and immensity of the universe as taught by Newton, and a new sense of man's relation to man and to the universe itself. The deists were altogether aware of this, and it was reflected in their prayers—prayers which by the very nature of deism had to be individual. But even in the writings of the reputed atheists—Diderot and others—we find prayers, running counter to some of our widely accepted notions about the beliefs and the thinking of these men.

In this climate of cultural fermentation, Jean-Jacques Rousseau, both philosophe and religionist or believer, occupies a special place. He was, after all, to become the great eighteenth-century French advocate of the individual conscience, of stern ethical principles, and of the future life, for he was a firm believer in Providence. With Jean-Jacques, reason was important, but it was, more often than not, linked with feeling or sentiment. Many of his writings were thereby in accord with the rising urge for sentimental values and for giving expression to the needs of the heart too long repressed. This trend became noticeable in the middle of the century and prevailed toward the end—a forerunner of the Romantic mood.

Baudelaire, in his *Intimate Journals*, looked upon prayer as "one of the great forces of intellectual dynamism,"[2] and, indeed, the theme of prayer could be worthy of attention and study since prayers recur in Rousseau as well as in writings of many great authors down through the ages. The factors mentioned above make the subject of prayer particularly fascinating when studied in the works of an eighteenth-century French writer. The present study purports to highlight certain aspects of Rousseau heretofore overlooked or believed non-existent because they are submerged and scattered throughout his writings

---

[2]   Charles Baudelaire, *Intimate Journals* (London: The Blackamore Press, New York: Random House, 1930), p. 43.

and also because an age of presumed enlightenment is often viewed as antagonistic to prayer. Questions on the subject immediately come to mind: what type or types of prayer are involved? What meaning do they hold? What is their format and content? What, basically, do they express? Since this study is written in English, we shall give all the prayers and quoted comments in English translation and reserve for the footnote the original French in which they were written. Translations of all prayers and other excerpts are this author's unless otherwise indicated, in which cases existing partial translations have been utilized and edited whenever found necessary.

The main part of this inquiry will be devoted to deistic prayers in Rousseau. Hence, a brief study of deism is now in place.

CHAPTER II

Deism:
Concept of Natural Religion

A. English Deism

1. Historical Background

Deism as an active movement of religious thought taken seriously for its intellectual challenge and causing widespread discussions and polemics lasted about one century. Its birthplace was England and its first major personality was John Toland whose *Christianity Not Mysterious* appeared in 1696, two years after the Licensing Act was not renewed and, therefore, a somewhat larger measure of freedom of expression prevailed. This great deistic debate subsided in England with the lukewarm response to Middleton's *Free Inquiry* in 1748, his demise in 1750, and the death of Henry Saint-John, first Viscount of Bolingbroke, in 1751. Remarkable enough as one of the quirks of history is the fact that after deism declined in England, it began to assume for the next half a century a vital role in French thought and literature.

2. Definition

Professor Torrey provides us with an excellent definition of deism "as consisting in the acceptance of a natural religion based on the common ideas of morality and including the worship of an impersonal deity whose laws are plain and engraved in the hearts of men, as opposed to revealed religions with their supernatural doctrines and specific religious duties."[1]

3. Herbert's Five Fundamental Beliefs

A precursor of deism in England is Edward Herbert, later known as Lord Herbert of Cherbury, and dubbed "the father of deism." He is best known for his deist work *De veritate*, published in Paris in 1624. Now, in general, all deists believe that natural religion antedates all historic religions, that natural religion, in fact, constitutes the core of the various religions, the common denominator present in all religions. Lord Herbert offered five of these fundamental truths that he calls "Common Notions,"[2] none of which is attained through revelation but is innate in man. They make more explicit Professor Torrey's pithy definition and we list them briefly: the belief in a Supreme Being, the need for His worship, the pursuit of a pious and virtuous life as the most important part of religious practice, the need of repentance for sins to become reconciled with God, and reward and punishment in the next world.

Among the major, better known and more militant English deists, in addition to precursor Lord Herbert who was not known as a deist in his day, we find: John Toland, *Christianity Not Mysterious*,1696, Lord Shaftesbury, *Letter Concerning Enthusiasm*, 1708, Matthew Tindal, *Christianity as Old as Creation*, 1730, which came to be called "the deists' Bible," Anthony Collins, *A Discourse of Free-Thinking*, 1713, Thomas Woolston, *A Defence of the Discourses on Miracles*, 1729, Conyers Middleton, *Free Inquiry Into the Miraculous Powers, Which Are Supposed to Have Subsisted in the Christian Church, From the Earliest Ages through Several Successive Centuries*, 1748, and Viscount Bolingbroke, *Letters on the Study and Use of History*, written in 1738 and published posthumously in 1754.

Obviously, these writers were not all of the same view and did not manage then to organize a religious denomination of their own. Hence, we cannot refer to a single work as containing the sum total of

---

[1] Norman L. Torrey, *The Spirit of Voltaire* (New York: Russell and Russell, 1938, reprinted 1968), *p. 228.*

[2] Peter Gay, *Deism: An Anthology* (Princeton, N.J.: D. Van Nostrand, 1968), p. 30.

deistic beliefs. Still, what they all share in common is a positive attitude to natural religion and a negative attitude toward the religions
in which they lived: Catholicism as well as the Anglican Church and
fundamental Protestantism. Historically, deism was the last link in a
chain of thought that began with the English Reformation substitut-
ing the authority of the Bible for that of the Catholic Church. Now,
"most of the advocates of the deistic philosophy in England contented
themselves with setting forth the tenets of the religion of nature without seeking an authoritative foundation for them in the Biblical revelation . . . , [In its stead] they asserted that the basis of authority was
to be found in reason and in the rational beliefs, common to all men,
to which it universally led."[3]

B. French Deism

I. Historical Background

We are familiar with the two trends that run concurrently in French
civilization and literature: one the Greco-Roman tradition and the
other, the religious tradition of Jewish and Christian origins. Before
long in the eighteenth century, an earlier developed intellectual
movement of a religious nature gains prominence under the name of
deism. It regards traditional religion in a negative manner.
Manuscripts of deistic works circulate clandestinely. One of them,
first published around 1750, was the anonymous *Pensées sur la religion
dont on cherche de bonne foy l'éclaircissement*, known also as *Doutes sur la
religion* and *Examen de la religion*. What one finds in this work is
mainly a deism of the critical type, with attacks on the historicity of
Scripture and such doctrines as the Trinity, original sin and
redemption. It maintains that true religion is founded on reason and
on the "golden rule." A similar work called *Analyse de la religion
chrétienne*, attributed to Dumarsais, was also passed about secretly
during the same period. However, French deism attained its full

---

[3]   Herbert M. Morais, *Deism in Eighteenth-Century America*, issued as Columbia
     University dissertation in 1934 and printed in New York. (Russell and Russell,
     1960), pp. 30–31.

growth only with Voltaire and Rousseau and, of course, the Encyclopedists.[4]

2. Transplantation and Its Consequences

Deism was, as we have seen, an outgrowth of English thought and characteristically British. So when it was taken up elsewhere there were, as might be expected, substantial changes. For instance, French deism assumed an anti-clerical stance and could lead to atheism. A case in point is that of Diderot. Early in his career, he had drawn his inspiration from Shaftesbury and was committed to a more emotional deism. When he wrote his *Pensées philosophiques* in 1746, he still subscribed to the deistic convictions of his youth. However, by 1749, his *Lettre sur les aveuqles* already reveals his break with deism and his embracing of atheism. He had shifted not to the mechanistic atheism of d'Holbach whose circle he frequented but to his own brand of atheism, stemming from a vitalistic determinism in the wake of biological speculations in the 1740's. The change did not occur, as was thought previously, in 1769, when he wrote his *Rêve de d'Alembert*, but twenty years earlier, in 1749, in the *Lettre sur les aveuqles*, as proven by Aram Vartanian and other scholars, and in the *Rêve*, Diderot merely hardened his position leading it to materialism: "What emerged finally, imaginatively synthesized, was an evolutionary materialism which proved to be one of the great scientific and philosophical movements of the eighteenth century."[5] Let us add that the Catholic Church in France, at that time, did not recognize fine distinctions among heretics, deists and atheists, and the works of all three were burned by the official executioner.

3. Voltaire and Rousseau

Both Voltaire and Rousseau, though they have reached deism in France on their own, owed a great deal of inspiration to England. Rousseau had gone to England in 1765 when he was in his early fifties

---

[4]   R. Z. L[auer], *New Catholic Encyclopedia*, 1967, IV, 723.

[5]   Aram Vartanian, "From Deist to Atheist: Diderot's Philosophical Orientation, 1746–1749," *Diderot Studies*, ed. Otis E. Fellows and Norman L. Torrey (Syracuse, N.Y.: Syracuse University Press, 1949), I, 61.

in order to escape expulsion and persecution. We know that he stayed at the home of the philosopher David Hume and, after their quarrel, went to Wootton to the home of M. Davenport, returning to France in1767. Voltaire had dwelled there, early in his career, for three years (1726–1729) and English society helped him crystallize his thinking on deism as on other matters. Being a friend of Bolingbroke, he was well exposed to meeting and discussing deism with those who subscribed to it. Later, he disseminated his ideas with the force of his keen intellect and masterful ability to write, so that he reached out to wider audiences than did his British friends.

Moreover, France was more receptive to deism and had a more fertile cultural soil for its full development than England. For the logical French mind, averse to compromise, pushed the abstract principles to their utmost logical conclusions while the British, being more pragmatic, were motivated by practical considerations. Besides, in France as in most continental Europe, the Church was identified with the old *régime* and conservatism and was inimical to new ideas. Deism therefore became anti-clerical and, in its most radical form, aimed at replacing the dogmatic theology of the Church with its own undogmatic religious ideology. As Pomeau puts it: "Voltaire strives to establish that deism is indeed a religion in the same way as the others and better than the others."[6] He will utilize his caustic satire and biting irony mercilessly in order to achieve his goal of *écraser l'infâme* while Diderot, as we have already seen, represents the extreme evolution of thought from deism to materialism.

In this ideational framework, Rousseau played a unique role. For "the tendency to a bare materialism was to some extent checked by the influence of Rousseau who was at once the product and the champion of a reaction against the stiffness and coldness of a cramped rationalism. In the fact that he thus represented the protest…against the bare negations of materialism is to be found the explanation of his wide popularity.[7]

---

[6] René Pomeau, *La Religion de Voltaire* (Paris: Nizet, 1956), p. 216.
[7] G.C. J[oyce], *Encyclopedia of Religion and Ethics*, 1928, IV 539.

4. Deism and Theism

According to many sources, the terms "deist" and "theist" were used interchangeably in the eighteenth century, especially among writers. Yet, Voltaire himself has no entry for "Deist" in his *Philosophical Dictionary*—perhaps due to the fact that the term was often associated in people's minds with atheism of which Voltaire was a persistent opponent. However, he does have an entry for "Theist" and this is, in part, what he says about it:

> The theist is a man firmly convinced of the existence of a Supreme Being, as good as He is powerful, who has created all the extended, vegetating, feeling and reflecting beings; who perpetuates their species, who punishes crime without cruelty and rewards, virtuous acts with kindness.
>
> The theist does not know how God punishes, how He protects, how He forgives; for he is not rash enough to flatter himself that he knows how God acts; but he knows that God does act and that He is just. The difficulties in the notion of Providence do not shake him in his faith, because they are only great difficulties and not disproofs; he submits himself to this Providence, although he merely perceives some of its effects and externals; and, judging things that he does not see by the things that he does see, he thinks that this Providence reaches into every place and time.[8]

We find a similar attitude in Rousseau too. In his *Letter to Voltaire on Providence* (1756), he speaks of "the theist"[9] who bases his sentiments only on probabilities. Moreover, at the beginning of the second part of the "*Profession of Faith of the Savoyard Vicar,*" (1762) he refers specifically to "theism or natural religion."[10] Here, he complains that Christians confuse "theism" with atheism or irreligion which is the directly opposite doctrine. It seems then safe to say that, generally speaking, people made no clear distinction between "deism" and "theism" as we do now, and what is more, they associated those terms with their opposites. This, however, may not have been true of the *élite*. Commenting on the term "theism" mentioned by the young interlocutor to the Savoyard Vicar, Ronald Grimsley says: "Philosophers and theologians of the eighteenth century already distin-

---

[8]   Voltaire, *Dictionnaire philosophique* (Paris: Garnier, 1961), p. 399. See also *Philosophical Dictionary*, trans. Peter Gay (New York: Basic Books, 1962), 11, 479.

[9]   Jean-Jacques Rousseau, *Lettre à Voltaire sur la Providence*, O.C. IV, 1070.

[10] Jean-Jacques Rousseau, *Profession de foi du vicaire savoyard*, in *Emile*, O.C. 606.

guished between 'theism' and 'deism': the former involved the establishment of a personal relationship between man and God through
the exercise of his natural powers and usually implied the acceptance
of Providence and immortality; deism, on the other hand, was a more
intellectual form of belief, stressing the idea that although God made
the world, he was no longer concerned with it or man's fate. According to this distinction, Rousseau would be a theist and Voltaire a deist.[11] Grimsley also admits what we said above, that the two terms
were often used indiscriminately by writers who were not interested
in theological distinctions.

By Grimsley's fine definition of the two terms, by Rousseau's use
of the term "theist" in his writings to qualify his views, and also by
the fact that Rousseau, especially under emotional strain but not exclusively, resorts to an appeal to a personal God, in addition to expressions of belief in Providence and in immortality, it appears to us
that Jean-Jacques can best be described as a theist rather than a pure
deist. That, of course, does not preclude the presence in his theism of
essential elements it shares with deism, such as the absence of Christological references in his prayers, including those of incarnation, of
Trinity, of original sin and its corollary the need of redemption, as
well as the use made of reason in religion, though complemented in
the case of Jean-Jacques with belief in conscience which, to him, is an
innate feeling and the supreme arbiter.

5. Rousseau—A Noahide?

The natural religion of which Voltaire and Rousseau speak, Professor
Torrey reminds us, "was considered as old as creation and enhanced
the favorite heroes of the deists, Confucius, Socrates and Cicero."[12] It
was the original religion, the *Ursprunq* religion, preceding the historic
religions. It comprises the core of religion which is common to all
religions that followed it. The writers on deism have thus
reconstructed abstractly and retroactively this original core-religion
and coined the term "deism" or "theism" for it. To students of

---

[11] Ronald Grimsley, *Jean-Jacques Rousseau—Religious Writings* (Oxford: Clarendon
Press, 1970), pp. 166–67, note 4.

[12] Cf. Torrey, *Voltaire and the English Deists*, p. 1.

Judaism, however, it is common knowledge that such a universal religion "as old as creation" did and does in fact exist. It is called Noahism or the religion of the descendants of Noah. As its name indicates, it originated with Noah, father of mankind, who, subsequent to the flood, received seven basic commandments indicated at the beginning of Genesis and referred to by the Talmud as "the seven commandments (or precepts) of the descendants of Noah." These constitute the quintessence of religion, the minimum of religion if you wish, the universal religion of mankind. Their source is revelation. Yet, they are also easily accepted by reason and one could hardly claim to be civilized without subscribing to them. They comprise one positive precept—justice—to which, incidentally, the deists, too, have assigned utter preponderance, and six negative precepts. They are, as recorded in the Talmud: 1) the promotion of justice, 2) the prohibition of blasphemy, 3) of idolatry, 4) of immorality, 5) of bloodshed, 6) of robbery, 7) of eating flesh from a living animal (humane treatment of animals).[13]

These commandments are regarded by Judaism as the foundation of all human, moral living. They are universal, applicable to and binding on all human beings. Given at the very beginning of the Bible, they clearly indicate the concern of the Divine Creator for all of humanity. What followed later, with Abraham and Moses, is the special creation and training of the Jewish people in moral, ethical and holy living through a detailed code of laws, with the purpose of being an example and a blessing and devoting life to service of all of mankind, of all of God's children.

In an autobiographical book on his spiritual journey, a former young French Catholic theological student, Aimé Pallière, discloses how the Italian rabbi whom he had consulted dissuaded him from becoming a proselyte to Judaism and, instead, suggested that he practice Noahism. Said Rabbi Elijah Benamozegh in a letter to Pallière: "The religion of humanity is no other than Noahism, not that it was instituted by Noah, but because it dates from the covenant made by

---

[13]　Talmud, tractate of *Sanhedrin*, p. 56a. Cf also Aaron Lichtenstein, *The Seven Laws of Noah*, 1981. Z. Berman Books. Publishers and Distributor. Brooklyn, N.Y.

God with humanity in the person of this just man. Here is the religion preserved by Israel to be transmitted to the Gentiles."[14]

Jean-Jacques, in his search for religious truth, has come across some Jews unlearned in Judaism about whom the Savoyard Vicar generalizes: "The Jews understand Hebrew no longer."[15] This could perhaps be true in the pre-emancipation period of the Jews, though we might also add that in the eighteenth century, the great seats Jewish scholarship had shifted to Eastern Europe. Another point the Vicar (i.e. Rousseau) makes is that he had tried to talk to Jews about what Judaism teaches but the Jews were vary circumspect, fearing persecution: "Those among us who are within reach to converse with Jews are hardly more advanced. These unfortunate people feel that they are in our arbitrary power; the tyranny that is exerted toward them renders them apprehensive . . ."[16] Rousseau sympathized with them and—this makes him a non-Jewish forerunner of modern religious Zionism—he envisaged the possibility of Jews having a free state of their own where they could discuss matters freely and securely, so that the world might know what they stand for. In Rousseau's words: "I will never believe that I have really heard the point of view of the Jews till they have a free State, with schools and universities of their own wherein they could speak and debate without any risk. Only then could we know what they have to say.[17]

Speaking earlier about religion, the Savoyard Vicar had said critically: "He who begins by choosing for Himself one single people and

---

[14] Aimé Pallière, *The Unknown Sanctuary*, trans. Louise Waterman Wise (New York: Bloch, 1928), pp. 134–35. See also Elie Benamozegh, *Israël et L'Humanité* (Paris: Ernest Leroux, 1914), especially the third part on "Mosaïsme et Noahisme." Cf. Prof. Nahum Rakover, *Law and the* Noahides. The Library of Jewish law, 1998. Deputy Attorney General of the State of Israel. Attempt to elucidate the Noahide obligation to establish a just legal system.

[15] Cf. *Profession de foi du vicaire savayard*, O.C. IV, 619: "Lss Juifs n'entendent plus l'hébreu."

[16] Ibid., pp. 620–21: "Ceux d'entre nous qui sont à portée de converser avec des Juifs ne sont guère plus avancés. Les malheureux se sentent à notre discrétion; la tyrannie qu'on exerce envers eux les rend craintifs…"

[17] Ibid., pp. 620–21: 'Je ne croirai jamais avoir bien entendu les raisons das Juifs, qu'ils n'aient un Etat libre, des écoles, des universités, où ils puissent parler et disputer sans risque. Alors seulement nous pourrons savoir ce qu'ils ont à dire."

proscribes the rest of mankind is not the common Father of all men; He who destines to eternal punishment the largest number of His creatures is not the merciful and good God that my reason has shown to me.[18] "This objection about eternal punishment to a majority of mankind is, of course, based on a teaching that is exclusively Christian. Judaism, probably unbeknown to him, conceives of all punishment as limited and aimed at expiation and redemption. As to the first objection, had Jean-Jacques been aware of Noahism and its affirmation of Divine solicitude for all of mankind (the direct opposite of proscription to which he objects), he would have been struck by the similarity between these Jewish teachings and his own to which he had arrived after much struggle and anguish. He would have found, in fact, a religion—Noahism—as old as creation. Then, most probably, Jean-Jacques would have also listed among his favorite heroes those who appeared in yonder antiquity: Noah and Moses. Furthermore, far from being doomed, those who, like Rousseau, abide by the seven universal principles are, in Jewish tradition, subject to salvation. As codified by Maimonides: "The righteous of the nations of the world have a share in the world to come."[19]

6. Deism and Prayer

Deism and theism are often regarded as synonyms and interchangeable. It is commonly believed that prayer has no place in either of them. Prayer is the language of religion, enabling man to communicate with God. On the other hand, deism and, by proximity, theism are believed to conceive of Deity as so far removed from man

---

[18]   Ibid., pp. 613–14.

[19]   Moses Maimonides, *Mishneh Torah* (Code of Jewish Law), "Laws of Repentance", chap. 3, end of law 5, and "Laws of Kings", chap. 8, law 11.

as to preclude communication. Yet, we do find prayers in Jean-Jacques as we do also among other standard-bearers of the eighteenth century. What type of prayers are they? What do they express? These and related questions constitute the subject of the present study.

CHAPTER III

Rousseau, Liturgical Prayers and Psalms

Jean-Jacques was born on June 28, 1712 in Geneva, the new Zion, the small Calvinist Zion, the holy city, where he attended services regularly and where impiety was also a civil offense. He did not need, it seems, these external promptings, for he had natural sensitivity and was naturally inclined toward spiritual expression, conditioned, no doubt, by the loss of his mother at his birth and, somewhat later, abandonment by his father. This is also evidenced in a letter written by Rousseau in a relaxed style on January 15, 1769, some nine years before his death, to a M. de Franquières who had requested guidance about his religious doubts: "I cannot form an opinion of the state of doubt you describe, since I have never experienced it. In my childhood, my belief was based on authority, in my youth on feeling, in my mature years on reason; now I believe because I have always believed."[1] Grimsley notes: "For Rousseau belief, not doubt, is man's natural inclination."[2] Prayer, the language of religion, can then be expected to have been part of Rousseau's life.

---

[1] Cf. *Lettre à M. de Franquières*, O.C. IV, 1134: "Je ne puis juger de cet état [de doute] parce qu'il n'a jamais été le mien. J'ai cru dans mon enfance par autorité, dans ma jeunesse par sentiment, dans mon âge mûr par raison; maintenant je crois parce que j'ai toujours cru." See also Jean Guéhenno, *Jean-Jacques Rousseau*, trans. John and Doreen Weightman (London: Routledge and Kegan Paul, New York: Columbia University Press, 1966), II, 232.

[2] Cf.Grimsley, *Reliqious Writings*, p. 382, note 1. See also O.C. IV, 1070–71, *Lettre à Voltaire sur la Providence* (1756): "Quand ma raison flotte, ma foi ne peut rester longtemps en suspens et se décide sans elle." See also O.C. IV, 567 in the *Profession de foi du vicaire savoyard* (1762): "Cet état [d'incertitude et de doute] est peu fait pour durer, il est inquiétant et pénible," rejecting doubt as a permanent

Jean-Jacques was in his youth a steady and receptive worshiper at Calvinist churches in Geneva where the singing of psalms occupied a prominent part in the liturgy. The prayers were easily understood as the vernacular French was used in the service and might have conditioned him to the idea of expressing praise and gratitude to Divinity. They equally made him aware of the central importance of good deeds,[3] since "man's duty to praise God not only in words but far more in his daily activities is the dominant keynote in the Psalms."[4] In addition to their all-pervading stress on "the ethical essence of Divine nature . . . not as an abstract doctrine but as an inspiration of man's living,"[5] Rousseau found in them also expressions of suffering, of pardon, of confession of sin, and especially of consolation which was so important to him. Some of Rousseau's key-concepts ("idées maîtresses"), such as the accessibility of God to every man without intermediaries, his penchant for absolute unity of God and finding

---

attitude. In the third promenade of *Les Rêveries du promeneur solitaire* (written between 1776 and 1778 and published posthumously in 1782), *O.C.* I, 1016, he says that the *philosophes* had "shaken" ("inquiété") and "disturbed" him ("ébranlé"), without ever persuading him ("sans m'avoir jamais convaincu"').

Cf. also Ronald Grimsley, *Rousseau and the Religious Quest* (Oxford: Clarendon Press, 1968), p. 40: "His dissatisfaction with contemporary philosophy does not mean that he himself is content to adopt an attitude of mere scepticism. From both the personal and the intellectual standpoint, he rejects the possibility of doubt as a permanent human attitude; man has an irresistible urge to know certain truths about himself and the world, and Rousseau is always keenly aware of this need....Rousseau professes himself incapable of understanding how anyone can be a sceptic *par système.*"

[3] For Rousseau's emphasis on ethics rather than dogma, cf. *Letter to M. de Franquières,* *O.C.* IV, 1137: "Je pense que chacun sera jugé non sur ce qu'il a cru, mais sur ce qu'il a fait." See also end of *Profession de foi,* *O.C.* IV, 635: "Ce qui importe à l'homme est de remplir ses devoirs sur la terre." (Compare also with end of *Ecclesiastes,* xii.13: "The end of the matter, all having been heard: fear God and keep His commandments; for this is the whole man"). See also in Grimsley, *Religious Writings,*. "Lettre à d'Alembert sur les spectacles" (1758), p. 77: "Monsieur, jugeons les actions des hommes, et laissons Dieu juger de leur foi."

[4] *The Psalms,* Hebrew text, English translation and commentary; edited by The Rev. Dr. A. Cohen (Hinhead, Surrey: The Soncino Press, 1945), Introduction, p. xii.

[5] Ibid.

God in nature[6] are certainly indigenous to the Psalms. Both the music—and Rousseau was always a music lover, considering it for a long time as his vocation and writing the article on music in the *Encyclopédie*—and the words must have left indelible marks on him. The Rousseau specialist, Pierre-Maurice Masson, writes: "However alluring that old music of the Psalms might have been, it would still have been powerless on the soul without the words that it made sing. Prayers of adoration, of submission and of gratefulness, fervent and humble wails, songs of triumphant joy—nowhere, perhaps, in the Bible, have the intimacy of man with God, the trust of the oppressed upright man, the certainty of Providential revenge, been rendered in stronger and more moving language. If spontaneous prayer ever came to the lips of Jean-Jacques, to the lips of the old man still more than to those of the adolescent—it must have been the prayer of the Psalms."[7] The following are some of the excerpts of the Psalms used by Rousseau:

> Strive, O Lord, with them that strive with me;
> Fight against them that fight against me.
> Take hold of shield and buckler,
> And rise up to my help.
> Draw out also the spear, and the battle-axe, against them that pursue me;
> Say unto my soul: "I am thy salvation!"
>
> xxxv. 1–3.

---

[6]   Ibid., Examples: Psalm xix, p. 53, first part: On the marvels of creation ("The heavens declare the glory of God, And the firmament showeth His handiwork"), and Psalm civ, p. 337: God's majesty recorded in nature, of which the eighteenth-century scientist, Alexander von Humboldt, wrote: "A single Psalm, the 104th, may be said to present a picture of the entire cosmos. . . . We are astonished to see within the compass of a poem of such small dimension, the universe, the heavens and the earth, thus drawn with a few grand strokes." But, adds Dr. Cohen in his commentary," behind the material universe, with its marvels and beauties, the Hebrew poet discerned the creative might of God. His meditation upon God's works impels him to praise the Maker." Cf. Grimsley, *Religious Quest*, p. 67: Rousseau "is not concerned primarily with understanding the universe but with entering into communion with its Creator." A quote from the *Profession of Faith* follows in Grimsley: "Je médite sur l'ordre de l'univers, non pour l'expliquer par de vains systèmes, mais pour l'admirer sans cesse, pour adorer le sage Auteur qui s'y fait sentir."

[7]   Pierre-Maurice Masson, *La Religion de Jean-Jacques Rousseau*, 2nd. ed. (Paris: Librairie Hachette, 1916), I, 33.

. . . .

But the Lord hath been my higher tower,
And my God the rock of my refuge.
And He hath brought upon them their own iniquity,
And will cut them off in their own evil;
The Lord our God will cut them off.

xciv.22–23.

. . . .

It is better to take refuge in the Lord
Than to trust in man.
It is better to take refuge in the Lord
Than to trust in princes.[8]

cxviii.8–9.

---

[8]   Cf. *The Psalms*, pp. 103, 311, 390 respectively. The text of Rousseau was the French translation by Marot and Bèze which has some variations in nuance from the original Hebrew, due partly to their observance of rhyme. In general, however, we find the French faithful to the original Hebrew in ideas and also meaningful because of the clear, modern language used. To assess their effect on Rousseau, we feel it worthwhile to give here the very text he used, as recorded by Masson, I, 33–34:

Rends confus mes accusateurs,
Et poursuis mes persécuteurs,
Prends, ô Dieu, prends, pour ma défense,
Le bouclier, l'épée, la lance.
Parle à mon âme en sa frayeur,
Et lui dis: je suis ton Sauveur.

xxxv.1–3.

Mais le Dieu fort, ce juste juge,
Est mon rocher, est mon refuge.
Il punira tous les forfaits,
L'Eternel les accablera ....

xciv.22–23.

. . . .

Il vaut mieux avoir confiance
En l'Eternel qu'en l'homme vain;
Il vaut mieux avoir confiance
En Dieu qu'en nul pouvoir humain.

cxviii.8–9.

Observes Masson: "This is the very wail of persecuted Rousseau; and it is also his hope. In proportion as the 'league' becomes more furious against him, his trust will affirm itself more invincible in the Providence of the upright which redresses eventually all the iniquities. At the bottom of this serene faith—and giving it all its robustness and its plenitude—I find again, more or less consciously accepted, the promises of the Genevan Psalter."[9]

Among the Psalms used in Geneva at religious services and collected by Masson (see above), we have Psalms xxxv, xciv and cxviii. Most revealingly, their themes have all had a personal relevance in Rousseau's life and Rousseau must have derived from them a measure of comfort. Thus Psalm xxxv is a "Prayer under Persecution" which expresses "a cry of distress from David when he was being haunted by Saul."[10] Psalm xciv is a "Plea for Divine Judgment . . . a state of moral chaos prevails in which justice is denied to those who need its protection most."[11] This psalm ends with the vindication of the righteous and the doom of the unjust. Psalm cxviii is one of "National Thanksgiving" and expresses "the feelings of gratitude which animated the hearts of the people . . . who ascribed the frustration of the plots of their enemies to the direct interposition of God."[12]

Masson has noted that in Rousseau's future confidence in a just Providence which redresses wrongs "I find again, more or less consciously accepted, the promises of the Genevan Psalter." Grimsley, too, concurs and writes: "He never completely escaped from the influence of his early environment."[13]

---

[9] Cf. Masson, *La Religion de Jean-Jacques Rousseau*, I, 34. See also Charly Guyot, *De Rousseau à Marcel Proust* (Neuchâtel: Editions Ides et Calendes, 1968), p. 28: "Dans son *Dictionnaire de Musique*, article 'Unité de mélodie,' Rousseau écrira: 'Lorsque j'entends chanter un psaume à quatre parties, je commence toujours par être saisi, ravi de cette harmonie pleine et nerveuse; et les premiers accords, quand ils sont entonnés bien juste, m'émeuvent jusqu'à frissonner.'"

[10] Cf. *The Psalms*, p. 103.

[11] Ibid., p. 308.

[12] Ibid., pp. 389–90.

[13] Cf. Grimsley, *Religious Writings*, p. 1.

"I Wanted to Become a Clergyman"

Albert Schinz in his analysis of "Les origines personnelles de la pensée religieuse de Rousseau" by Giraud says that Giraud tries to dissociate Rousseau from the *philosophes* and quotes him as speaking of Calvinists with real sympathy: "Rousseau is by nature a religious soul; two centuries of Protestant heredity have put into his heart the need to believe, to pray, to adore; he owes this fundamental disposition to his ancestors who have not lived in vain in the severe *mystique* of Calvin. . . . Voltaire was born an unbeliever, Rousseau was born a believer."[1]

Deserving of attention at this point are the early signs of Rousseau's potential vocation which he thought to be the clergy. We know that, at the age of ten, Jean-Jacques was entrusted to the care of M. Lambercier, a country clergyman who was reputedly as wise as he was religious and whom Rousseau recollected later in life in the *Confessions* as a man of discreet and reasonable attitudes toward the religious upbringing of his pupils and also as one in whose home he had found perfect happiness.[2] In the pious home of that pastor and his conscientious sister at Bossey, George Havens tells us, "young Rousseau listened attentively to the daily reading aloud of the Bible at family prayers, took into his being the sonorous rhythm of the oriental phrases with their mysterious imagery, heard the resounding oratory of sermons on Sunday vigorously excoriating sin or exhorting earnestly to good conduct, and so little by little formed the basically

---

[1]   Albert Schinz, *La Pensée religieuse de Rousseau et ses récents interprètes* (Paris: Librairie Félix Alcan, 1927), p. 35.

[2]   Cf.Grimsley, *Religious Writings*, p. 1.

moralistic outlook which . . . remained with him throughout life as a bright ideal."[3] Two years later, when he returned to Geneva in 1724–5, he was taken care of by Gabriel and Théodora Bernard, his uncle and aunt, for a few months. Grimsley is convinced that "if adequate financial resources had been available, he would probably have been trained for the ministry.:[4] As the family debated what he should become, Jean-Jacques expressed his own preference in these terms: "I wanted to become a clergyman, because I thought it a fine thing to preach."[5] Financial considerations having made the studies for a religious calling impossible, Jean-Jacques was apprenticed to a brutal engraver instead, which led him to leave Geneva behind on Sunday, March 14, 1728, when he found the gates of the city locked. Soon afterwards, he converted to Catholicism. However, the idea of his vocation recurs—only this time as a priest, perhaps a village priest, some of Madame de Warens' friends wondered. Whereupon, he was sent off to a Lazarist seminary where, according to some, he stayed but two months and according to others five months. The net result was that he was judged unsuitable for the clergy and, therefore, in its stead, he was given some training as a musician.

Yet, it was going to be via the pen, as a writer, that Jean-Jacques would achieve greatness and become "the instructor of the human race for a whole society and a whole century."[6] And the foregoing review of his early life and experiences leads us not to be surprised to find in his writings, both the late and the early ones, a plethora of prayers and discussions on prayer as well as the tone of a moralist. These show that there was, after all, some basis for his consideration of the clergy as a vocation.

---

[3] George R. Havens, *The Age of Ideas* (New York: The Free Press, 1966), p. 236.

[4] Cf. Grimsley, *Religious Writings*, p. 2.

[5] Cf. Guéhenno, I, 12 quotes the original text of Rousseau: "J'aimais mieux être ministre, car je trouvais bien beau de prêcher."

[6] Cf. Guéhenno, I, 19.

CHAPTER V

Early Prayers of Adoration at Les Charmettes—Toward Deism

It was in the idyllic, rural life at Les Charmettes near Mme de Warens that Jean-Jacques found peace and serenity and tried to educate himself through the acquisition of a "storehouse of ideas." There, too, he prayed. In a striking passage of his *Confessions*, he reveals to us the close association of religious feeling with natural beauty. Rousseau writes:

> I rose every morning before the sun, and passed through a neighboring orchard into a pleasant path which, running above a vinyard, led toward Chambéry. While walking, I offered up my prayers—not by a vain motion of the lips, but a sincere elevation of my heart—to the Great Author of delightful Nature, whose beauties were spread out before me. I never liked to pray in a chamber; it seems to me that the walls and all the little workmanship of man interpose themselves between God and myself. I love to contemplate Him in His works, which elevate my soul and raise my thoughts to Him. My prayers were pure, I can affirm it and, therefore, worthy to be heard. I asked for myself, and her from whom my thoughts were never divided, only an innocent and quiet life, exempt from vice, sorrow and want; I prayed that we might die the death of the just, and partake of their lot hereafter. For the rest, it was rather admiration and contemplation than request, being satisfied that the best means to obtain what is necessary from the Giver of every perfect good is rather to deserve than to solicit. Returning from my walk, I lengthened the way by taking a roundabout path, still contemplating with earnestness and delight the beautiful scenes with which I was surrounded—those only objects that never fatigue either the eye or the heart.[1]

---

[1] *Les Confessions*, Book 6, O.C. I, 236: "Je me levais tous les matins avant le soleil. Je montais par un verger voisin dans un très joli chemin qui était au-dessus de la

We notice that Rousseau's praying was spontaneous and heartfelt. At the same time, we must agree with Ronald Grimsley that the religious fervor of Jean-Jacques was due to the beauty of nature rather than to the appeal of Jesus to whom no reference is made. This will become a pattern of behavior of Rousseau to look for emotional stimulation in nature and for direct communion with the spiritual power present in the universe. His stay at Les Charmettes certainly facilitated this need and this craving of his. Moreover, his feelings for Mme de Warens herself were also associated with his feelings for nature. Jean-Jacques writes: "I would see her everywhere amongst the flowers and the greenery; her charms and those of the spring were blended together in my eyes."[2] At the same time, his early experience with religion in Geneva could not be forgotten and the moralist comes to the fore: "My prayers were pure, I venture to say, and for that reason deserved to be heard." The wish, in the prayer, to die "the death of the just" reminds us of the exactly same wish and expression found in the Bible.[3]

In Rousseau's conception of prayer, formulated at Les Charmettes, we already discern deistic elements, such as: absence of any reference to Jesus, direct communication between man and his Crea-

---

vigne, et suivait la côte jusqu'à Chambéry. Là, tout en me promenant, je faisais ma prière qui ne consistait pas en un vain balbutiement de lèvres, mais dans une sincère élévation de coeur à l'auteur de cette aimable nature dont les beautés étaient sous mes yeux. Je n'ai jamais aimé à prier dans la chambre; il me semble que les murs et tous ces petits ouvrages des hommes s'interposent entre Dieu et moi. J'aime à le contempler dans ses oeuvres tandis que mon coeur s'élève à lui. Mes prières étaient pures, je puis le dire, et dignes par là d'être exaucées. Je ne demandais pour moi, et pour celle dont mes voeux ne me séparaient jamais, qu'une vie innocente et tranquille, exempte du vice, de la douleur, des pénibles besoins, la mort des justes, et leur sort dans l'avenir. Du reste, cet acte se passait plus en admiration et en contemplation, qu'en demandes, et je savais qu'auprès du dispensateur des vrais biens le meilleur moyen d'obtenir ceux qui nous sont nécessaires est moins de les demander que de les mériter. Je revenais en me promenant par un assez grand tour, occupé à considérer avec intérêt et volupté les objets champêtres dont j'étais environné, les seuls dont l'oeil et le coeur ne se lassent jamais." See also *"The Confessions"of Jean-Jacques Rousseau*, Preface by Edmund Wilson (New York: Alfred A. Knopf, 1923), I, 294–95.

[2] Ibid., Vol. I, Book 3, p. 105 and cf. Grimsley, *Religious Quest*, p. 7

[3] Pentateuch, Book of Numbers, xxiii.10.

tor, nature as one source of revealing God and inspiring man to reach God, with the corollary that nature is good ("this delightful nature"—"cette aimable nature"). On the other hand, we still find here petitionary elements ("I asked only") which he tries to play down by stressing that his main worship consisted of admiration and contemplation rather than of requests and, if not fully convinced that he has made his point, corroborates that the best means of obtaining the blessings he had prayed for is "to deserve rather than to solicit." Perhaps the fact that his conception of prayer at Les Charmettes was written up retroactively in the *Confessions* some thirty years later accounts for these "explanations."

As illustrations of this conception of prayer during his sojourn at Les Charmettes, we have in particular two long prayers in his own handwriting which were published for the first time in 1905 by the well-known scholar, Théophile Dufour, as "Pages inédites de Jean-Jacques Rousseau."[4] Masson calls them two great prayers which, though not sufficiently well-known, are, however, most beautiful and render, if one may speak thus, a unique sound in Rousseau's work.[5] While Masson believes they were written between Rousseau's twenty-fourth and twenty-eighth year, which means between 1736 and 1740, Dufour is more specific and dates them 1738 or 1739. The first prayer reads:

> We prostrate ourselves in Thy Divine presence, great God, Creator and Preserver of the universe in order to render to Thee the homage due to Thee, to thank Thee for all the kindnesses that Thou hast bestowed upon us and to address to Thee our humble prayers.
>
> Our Father, etc.
>
> We present to Thee, O my God, our homage and our adoration: deign to accept them. We are but dust and ashes in Thy sight and we ought to stand in Thy awesome presence only with fear and trembling, but Thy mercy is even greater than Thy majesty; we put our trust in Thy infinite clemency. Thou art our Creator and we are the product of Thy goodness; Thou art our Father, we are Thy children; regard favorably then and accept our earnest wishes, our prayers and our thanksgivings.

---

[4]   *Annales de la Société Jean-Jacques Rousseau* (Genève: Chez A. Jullien, 1905), Tome premier, "Pages inédites de Jean-Jacques Rousseau," Première série, par Théophile Dufour, pp. 221–29. See also *O.C.* IV, 1034–39.

[5]   Cf. Masson, *La Religion de Jean-Jacques Rousseau*, I, 120.

We thank Thee for all the favors, for all the blessings which Thou dost shower upon mankind, and especially for all those which we have received from Thee since birth; we thank Thee far having created us, for having endowed us with a rational soul, for having made us cognizant of Thy Divine nature, for having, through Thy holy Providence, provided for our needs in our wretchedness, and relieved our infirmities, and finally for having united us together.

Continue to bestow all these favors upon us, Almighty God, but never suffer us to misuse them; give us the knowledge and the will to serve Thee in the manner most pleasing to Thee; lead us always in the path of virtue, never allowing us to stray from it. Do not permit, O my God, that we ever be so unhappy as to make us doubt Thy Divine existence even momentarily; rouse in our hearts the love which we owe to Thy fatherly tenderness and all Thy kindnesses, the respect and the reverence that we owe to Thy immense majesty and to Thy awesome power, and the charity that we owe to our fellow-man. May Thy word be in our mouths, and may Thy law be in our hearts; bestow Thy holy blessing on our union; may it inspire in us a mutual desire to serve Thee. In one word, O my God, give us all that Thou knoweth we need to contribute to Thy glory and labor for our salvation.

For the Evening

Grant us also a sweet and calm night; we entrust our spirits and our bodies to Thy Divine protection.

For the Morning

Bless also our labor of this day and protect us, by Thy Divine Providence, from everything that could hurt us and, above all, from offending Thee.[6]

---

[6]
Cf. *Annales*, pp. 221–23. Ses also *O.C.* IV, 1034–35. See also Guéhenno, I, 72–73 for partial translation. The original follows:

Nous nous prosternons en votre présence divine, grand Dieu, créateur et conservateur de l'univers, pour vous rendre les hommages que nous vous devons, pour vous remercier de tous les bienfaits que nous avons reçus de vous et pour vous adresser nos humbles prières.

Notre- Père, etc.

Nous vous présentons, ô mon Dieu, nos hommages et nos adorations: daignez les agréer. Nous ne sommes que poudre et cendre devant vous, et ce n'est qu'en tremblant que nous devrions nous mettre en votre redoutable présence, rnais vous avez encore plus de miséricorde que de majesté; nous nous confions en votre clémence infinie. Vous êtes notre créateur, nous sommes l'ouvrage de votre bonté; vous êtes notre père, nous sommes vos enfants; recevez donc favorablement, ô mon Dieu, nos voeux, nos prières et nos actions de grâces.

Nous vous remercions de toutes les grâces et de tous les biens dont vous comblez les hommes, et en particulier de tous ceux que nous avons reçus de

As corroborating proof of the Rousseau authorship of this prayer, Dufour[7] cites its two allusions to the "union" of Mme de Warens and Jean-Jacques ("for having united us together" and "bestow Thy holy blessing on our union"). We also wish to add that certain key-concepts ("idées maîtresses") of Jean-Jacques do appear in this prayer anticipating their future repetition or development and constitute internal evidence of Rousseau's authorship of this prayer. Thus, the concept that "Thy mercy is even greater than Thy majesty" will be found again among other places in the *Letter to Voltaire on Providence* (1756) in these words: "Why do you wish to justify His omnipotence at the expense of His goodness? If one must choose between two errors, I prefer the first one."[8] Julie, too, will write in 1761: "The God I serve is a merciful God, a Father: what moves me most is His good-

---

vous dès notre naissance; nous vous remercions de nous avoir créés, de nous avoir doués d'une âme raisonnable, de nous avoir donné la connaissance de votre divinité, d'avoir pourvu, par votre sainte providence, aux besoins de notre misère et au soulagement de nos infirmités, et enfin de nous avoir unis l'un à l'autre.

Continuez-nous toutes ces grâces, Dieu tout puissant, mais ne permettez pas que nous en abusions jamais; donnez-nous les lumières et la volonté de vous servir de la manière qui vous est la plus agréable; conduisez-nous toujours dans le chemin de la vertu; ne permettez pas que nous nous en égarions jamais. Ne perrnettez pas, ô mon Dieu, que nous soyons jamais assez malheureux pour douter un seul moment de votre divine existence; excitez dans nos coeurs l'amour que nous devons à votre tendresse paternelle et à tous vos bienfaits, le respect et la vénération que nous devons à votre immense majesté; et à votre puissance redoutable, et la charité que nous devons à notre prochain. Que votre parole soit dans notre bouche et votre loi dans notre coeur; répandez votre sainte bénédiction sur notre union; qu'elle serve à nous exciter mutuellement à vous servir. En un mot, ô mon Dieu, donnez-nous tout ce que vous voyez qui nous est nécessaire pour contribuer à votre gloire et pour travailler à notre salut.

Pour le Soir
Donnez-nous aussi une nuit douce et tranquille: nous recommandons nos esprits et nos corps à votre divine protection.

Pour le Matin
Bénissez aussi notre travail de cette journée et nous garantissez, par votre divine providence, de tout ce qui pourrait nuire et principalement de vous offenser.

[7]   Cf. Dufour, *Annales*, p. 222, note.
[8]   Cf. *Lettre à Voltaire sur la Providence*, O.C. IV, 1061.

ness. . . . His power astonishes me. His immensity confounds me, His justice . . . Well . . . though He be just, He is merciful.[9] The same is true about rejection of doubt as a permanent state: "Do not permit, O my God, that we ever be so unhappy as to make us doubt Thy Divine existence even momentarily." In his *Letter to Voltaire on Providence*, Rousseau says similarly: "The state of doubt is too violent a state for my soul; when my reason wavers, my faith cannot remain long in suspense and [therefore] determines itself without it [i.e. reason]."[10] The Savoyard Vicar (1762) also tells his listener: "This state [of doubt] is little made to last, it is disquieting and painful."[11] Finally, in his *Letter to M. de Franquières* (1769), he writes: "I cannot form an opinion of that state [of doubt you describe], since I have never experienced it."[12] Grimsley describes this aspect of Rousseau's outlook by saying that "he stressed his overwhelming need to believe in God and the immortality of the soul as the only means of making life bearable."[13] Equally an emphasis typical of Jean-Jacques is the inclusion in this prayer of "the charity that we owe to our fellow-man," placing deeds above creed, as was discussed above in Chapter III of this inquiry. The concept that "Thy law be in our hearts" expresses a tenet of natural law that God's will is inscribed in the human heart rather than revealed in a book. Finally, the addendum for the morning prayer "bless also our labor of this day" seems to refer to his pursuits at Les Charmettes which he took seriously in his effort to overcome his lack of formal education.

This first prayer is termed by Masson[14] as one of adoration and general requests that can be addressed by any human being to the Creator and common Father, except for the passing references to "our union." It is a personal prayer in the tradition of Protestant Geneva where such prayers in the vernacular were part of the regular religious service and expressed the specific need of the day. Equally of

9 Cf. *Julie ou La Nouvelle Héloïse*, O.C., Vol. II, Part 6, Letter VIII, p. 696.
10 Cf. *Lettre à Voltaire sur la Providence*, O.C. IV, 1070–71.
11 Cf. *Profession de foi du vicaire savoyard*, O.C. IV, 567.
12 Cf. *Lettre à M. de Franquières*, O.C. IV, 1134.
13 Cf. Grimsley, *Religious Writings*, p. 30.
14 Cf. Masson, *La Religion de Jean-Jacques Rousseau*, I, 121.

Genevan origin[15] is the habit of intercalating in his personal prayer the official *Pater* prayer, "Our Father . . . ," as Rousseau does here between the first and second paragraphs. While Guéhenno, quoting the beginning of this prayer, finds that it "breathes tranquillity .and confidence" and "God appears as a beneficent Father,"[16] it seems to us that this beginning is but a mere introduction while the gist of the prayer is located toward the end of the second paragraph ("Thou art our Creator, we are the product of Thy goodness; Thou art our Father, we are Thy children"). Moreover, once Jean-Jacques prays and as early as the beginning of the second paragraph, what he voices are unworthiness and anxiety ("We are but dust and ashes in Thy sight, and we ought to stand in Thy awesome presence only with fear and trembling"). We do know that Rousseau, reading Jansenist writings, became upset about his salvation. Burgelin notes Rousseau's state of mind at that time by saying that it is common knowledge that, at the time these prayers were composed, fear of death and damnation caused Jean-Jacques to pass through a moment of deep crisis.[17] It would seem, therefore, that both sentiments are present in Rousseau and that he moves from concern to confidence when he underlines what to him is an *idée maîtresse*, namely that the Divinity's mercy is greater than His majesty. To be noted, too, in this first prayer, as in the second, which we will analyze soon is the absence of any reference to Jesus, though in the first prayer the thought of Jesus is present in the quoted *Pater Noster*. In their eagerness "to dissociate[18] Rousseau from the *philosophes*, "some writers, like Victor Giraud[19] (in *Les Origines personnelles de la religion de Rousseau*), tend to rationalize away the peripheral mention of mere passing reference to Christianity and, that

---

[15] Ibid., p. 127.

[16] Cf. Guéhenno, p. 72.

[17] Pierre Burgelin, *Jean-Jacques Rousseau et la religion de Genève* (Genève: Editions Labor et Fides, 1962; Paris: Diffusion en France, Librairie Protestante), p. 8.

[18] Cf. Albert Schinz, p. 35.

[19] Ibid., p. 36: "Victor Giraud raconte, en partie d'après Masson, comment Rousseau compose aux Charmettes deux prières qui, sans doute, 'n'ont rien de spécifiquement catholique, ni même de chrétien, puisque le nom et la pensée du Christ en sont absents,' mais qui ont l'accent religieux, les élans chaleureux d'un 'vrai croyant'; la foi y 'manque de précisions,' mais c'est qu'elle est 'plus sentimentale qu'intellectuelle,' ce qui est une compensation."

only in the first prayer, in order to, says their critic Albert Schinz, appropriate Rousseau as "an ally."[20] Others, like Masson, though having a similar aim according to Schinz, nevertheless admit that when Rousseau's "piety expresses itself freely, outside the traditional forms, it seems that Christ becomes unnecessary and that he has no more need of any intermediary to address himself to the "common Father of all." And Masson clearly admits that "Unconsciously perhaps, deism works itself out in him."[21]

The second prayer, written after difficulties with Mme de Warens, is much longer and, as Masson points out, it is more fervent and leads to self-examination and to making personal resolutions in which he puts his entire heart. The tone is grave, meditative and moving.[22] We believe it important to bring that second prayer here *in toto* in English translation as well as in the original French. Because of its length, the French original will be given in the text.

Omnipotent God, Eternal Father, my heart is uplifted in Thy presence to offer Thee therein the homage and the adoration due to Thee; my soul, penetrated with Thy immense majesty, Thy awesome power and Thy infinite grandeur, humbles itself before Thee with feelings of the deepest reverence and the most respectful obeisance. O my God, I adore Thee with the complete extent of my powers, I acknowledge Thee as the Creator, the Preserver, the Ruler and the absolute Sovereign of all that exists, the absolute and independent Being who has need of nothing else for His own existence, who has created everything by His power and without whose sustenance all beings would immediately return to nothingness. I acknowledge that Thy Divine Providence sustains and governs the entire universe, but these tasks, inspired by kindness, are incapable of altering in the least Thy awesome tranquillity. Finally, whatever magnificence prevails in the construction of this vast universe, I realize that to bring it out from nothingness in all its perfection required only one moment of Thy will and that, far from being the last endeavor of Thy might, all the vigor of the human spirit is not even capable of conceiving how much farther Thou couldst extend the effects of Thy infinite power. I stand in

---

[20]   Ibid., p. 3.

[21]   Cf.Masson, *La Religion de Jean-Jacques Rousseau*, I, 125.

[22]   Ibid., p. 121.

adoration of so much grandeur and majesty and since the feebleness of my understanding does not permit me to comprehend the full extent of Thy Divine perfection, my soul, filled with submission and respect, reveres its awesome and immense depth while recognizing itself incapable of fathoming it.

But, O God of Heaven, if Thy omnipotence is infinite, Thy Divine kindness is no less than that. O my Father, my heart takes delight in meditating on the greatness of Thy benefactions; it finds therein a thousand inexhaustible sources of zeal and blessings. What tongue could worthily enumerate all the gifts I have received from Thee? Thou hast created me from nothingness, Thou hast given me life, Thou hast endowed me with a rational soul, Thou hast engraved in the depth of my heart laws the execution of which Thou rewardest with eternal happiness—just and gentle laws, the practice of which will lead me to happiness, beginning even in this life. Thou hast imparted joys to my lot on this earth, and while exhibiting before my eyes the moving and magnificent spectacle of this vast universe, Thou didst not disdain to assign a great part of it for my comfort and pleasure. O sublime Benefactor, Thy kindnesses are as infinite as Thou art; Thou art the King of nature, but Thou art the Father of mankind. What hearts will sufficiently rouse themselves to express to Thee love and gratitude worthy of Thy kindness? My homage and my zeal, being so weak, will they dare to appear before Thee to satisfy my gratitude by their expression? Yes, my God, Thou condescendest to accept them out of regard for my weakness; Thou acceptest feelings far from being worthy of Thee, in truth, but they are, however, the fruit of all the efforts of my heart; my gratitude, my zeal and my love, feeble as they are, are not disdained by Thy Divine kindness. O my Creator, my heart is roused by the contemplation of all Thy favors and all Thy blessings: do accept them in Thy abundant mercy.

O my God, pardon all the sins which I have committed till this day, all the straying into which I have fallen; deign to have pity on my weaknesses, deign to destroy in me all the vices into which those weaknesses have led me. My conscience tells me how guilty I am; I feel that all those pleasures that my passions set before me when I strayed from the path of wisdom, are now worse than an illusion, and have turned into bitter and hateful memories; I feel that the only real pleasures are those we enjoy in practicing virtue and in carrying out the duties it prescribes. I am overwhelmed with regret for having made such poor use of a life and freedom which Thou hast granted me only to give me the means to render myself worthy of eternal bliss. Accept my repentance, O my God! Ashamed of my past faults, I firmly resolve to make up for them by a conduct of rectitude and sobriety. Henceforth, I shall relate all my actions to Thee, I shall meditate about Thee, I shall bless Thee, serve Thee and fear Thee. I shall always keep Thy law in my heart and shall practice it in all my deeds; I shall love my neighbor as myself; I shall render service to him in everything that depends on me, in matters affecting the body as in matters affecting the soul; I shall always remember that Thou desirest his happiness no less than mine; I shall have pity for the unfortunates and I shall help them with all my might; I shall endeavor to know well all the duties of my condition and I shall fulfill them with care. I shall bear in mind that Thou art witness to all my deeds and I shall endeavor to do nothing which is unworthy of Thy awesome presence. I shall be forgiving towards others and strict towards myself, I shall resist temptation, I shall live in purity, I shall be temperate and moderate in all things and I shall permit myself only those pleasures that virtue allows. Above all, I shall control my anger and my impatience and I shall try to behave gently towards everyone; I shall speak evil of no one, I shall permit myself neither rash judgment nor malevolent conjectures about the behavior of others; I shall detach myself, as much as possible, from the fads and fashions of the world, from the ease and comforts of life, to occupy myself solely with Thee and Thy infinite perfection. I shall wholeheartedly forgive all those who might offend me, just as I forgive now, unreservedly, those who may have offended me in the past: I pray Thee, O my God, to forgive them also and to grant them Thy favor. I shall avoid with care to ever offend anyone and, if I have this misfortune, I shall not feel ashamed to redress it in the most satisfactory manner. I shall always submit wholeheartedly to all that it will please Thy Divine Providence to order me to do, and I shall always accept with perfect submission to Thy supreme will all the blessings or the hardships that it will please Thee to send upon me. I shall prepare myself for death, as for the day when I have to render account of all my deeds, and shall await it without fear since it will deliver me from the tyranny of the body and unite me with Thee forever. In sum, O my Sovereign Ruler, I shall devote my life to serve Thee, to obey Thy laws and to fulfill my duties: I beseech Thy benedictions on these resolutions which I form with all my heart and with a firm purpose to carry them out, knowing, as I do, from sad experience that, without the help of Thy grace, the firmest decisions vanish, but that Thou never refusest Thy grace to those who ask Thee for it from the heart with humility and fervor.

I beseech similar grace, O my God, upon my dear mother, upon my dear benefactress and upon my dear father. Grant them, Father of mercies, all the help which they need, forgive them all the wrong they have done, inspire them with the good they ought to do and give them the strength to fulfill both the duties of their station in life and those that Thou requirest of them. Remember, in general, all my benefactors; reward them in kind for all the kindnesses which they have done to me; grant also the assistance of Thy Divine benedictions to all my friends, my country and mankind in general; remember, O my God, that Thou art the common Father of all mankind, and have pity upon us all in the abundance of Thy mercy.[23]

> Dieu tout puissant, Père éternel, mon coeur s'élève en votre présence, pour vous y offrir les hommages et les adorations qu'il vous doit; mon âme, pénétrée de votre immense majesté, de votre puissance redoutable et de votre grandeur infinie, s'humilie devant vous, avec les sentiments de la plus profonde vénération et du plus respectueux abaissement. O mon Dieu, je vous adore de toute l'étendue de mes forces, je vous reconnais pour le créateur, le conservateur, le maître et le souverain absolu de tout ce qui existe, pour l'être absolu et indépendant qui n'a besoin que [de] soi-même pour exister, qui a tout créé par sa puissance et sans le soutien duquel tous les êtres rentreraient aussitôt dans le néant. Je reconnais que votre divine providence soutient et gouverne le monde entier, sans que ces soins, pleins de bonté, soient capables d'altérer le moins du monde votre auguste tranquillité. Enfin, quelque magnificence qui règne dans la construction de ce vaste univers, je conçois qu'il n'a fallu, pour le sortir du néant dans toute sa perfection, qu'un instant de votre volonté et que, bien loin d'être le dernier effort de votre puissance, toute la vigueur de l'esprit humain n'est pas seulement capable de concevoir combien vous pourriez étendre au delà les effets de votre pouvoir infini. J'adore tant de grandeur et de majesté, et

---

[23]   Cf.Dufour, pp. 224–29. See also *O.C.* IV, 1036–39. See also partial translation in Guéhenno, I, 84–85.

puisque la faiblesse de mes lumières ne me permet pas de concevoir toute l'étendue de vos perfections divines, mon âme, pleine de soumission et de respect, en révère l'auguste et immense profondeur, se reconnaissant incapable de la pénétrer.

Mais, ô Dieu du ciel, si votre puissance est infinie, votre divine bonté ne l'est pas moins. O mon Père, mon coeur se plaît à méditer sur la grandeur de vos bienfaits; il y trouve mille sources intarissables de zèle et de bénédictions. Quelle bouche pourrait faire dignement l'énumération de tous les biens que j'ai reçus de vous? Vous m'avez tiré du néant, vous m'avez donné l'existence, vous m'avez doué d'une âme raisonnable, vous avez gravé dans le fond de mon coeur des lois à l'exécution desquelles vous avez attaché le prix d'un bonheur éternel, lois pleines de justice et de douceur et dont la pratique tend à me rendre heureux, même dès cette vie. Vous avez attaché des douceurs à mon sort sur cette terre, et en exposant devant mes yeux le spectacle touchant et magnifique de ce vaste univers, vous n'avez pas dédaigné d'en destiner une grande partie à ma commodité et à mes plaisirs. O sublime bienfaiteur, vos bienfaits sont infinis comme vous; vous êtes le Roi de la nature, mais vous êtes le père des humains. Quels coeurs s'enflammeront assez pour vous témoigner un amour et une reconnaissance dignes de vos bontés? Mes hommages et mon zèle, tout faibles qu'ils sont, oseront-ils se présenter à vous pour satisfaire à ma gratitude? Oui, mon Dieu, vous daignez les agréer, en considération de ma faiblesse; vous acceptez des sentiments bien indignes de vous, à la vérité, mais qui sont cependant le fruit de tous les efforts de mon coeur; ma reconnaissance, mon zèle et mon amour, tout faibles qu'ils sont, ne sont pas dédaignés de votre divine bonté. O mon créateur, mon coeur s'excite, par la contemplation de toutes vos grâces et de tous vos bienfaits, à vous offrir des actions de grâces et des remercîments proportionnés: agréez-le[s] dans la plénitude de votre miséricorde.

O mon Dieu, pardonnez tous les péchés que j'ai commis jusqu'à ce jour, tous les égarements où je suis tombé; daignez avoir pitié de mes faiblesses, daignez détruire en moi tous les vices où elles m'ont entraîné. Ma conscience me dit combien je suis coupable: je sens que tous les plaisirs que mes passions m'avaient représentés dans l'abandon de la sagesse sont devenus pour moi pires que l'illusion et qu'ils se sont changés en d'odieuses amertumes; je sens qu'il n'y a de vrais plaisirs que ceux qu'on goûte dans l'exercice de la vertu et dans la pratique de ses devoirs. Je suis pénétré de regret d'avoir fait un si mauvais usage d'une vie et d'une liberté que vous ne m'aviez accordées que pour me donner les moyens de me rendre digne de l'éternelle félicité. Agréez mon repentir, ô mon Dieu! Honteux de mes fautes passées, je fais une ferme résolution de les réparer par une conduite pleine de droiture et de sagesse. Je rapporterai désormais toutes mes actions à vous, je vous méditerai, je vous bénirai, je vous servirai, je vous craindrai; j'aurai toujours votre loi dans mon coeur et toutes mes actions en seront la pratique; j'aimerai mon prochain comme moi-même; je le servirai en tout ce qui dépendra de moi, tant par rapport au corps que par rapport à l'âme; je me souviendrai toujours que vous ne voulez pas moins son bonheur que le mien propre; j'aurai pitié des malheureux et je les secourrai de toutes mes forces; je tâcherai de bien connaître tous les devoirs de mon état et je les remplirai avec attention. Je me souviendrai que vous êtes témoin de toutes mes actions et je tâcherai de ne rien faire d'indigne de votre auguste présence. Je serai indulgent aux autres et sévère à moi-même, je résisterai aux tentations, je vivrai dans la pureté, je serai tempérant, modéré en tout, et je ne me permettrai jamais que les plaisirs autorisés par la vertu. Surtout je réprimerai ma colère et mon impatience, et je tâcherai de me rendre doux à l'égard de tout le monde; je ne dirai du mal de personne, je ne me permettrai ni jugements téméraires, ni mauvaises conjectures sur la conduite d'autrui; je me détacherai, autant qu'il me sera possible, du goût du monde, des aises et des commodités de la vie, pour m'occuper uniquement de vous et de vos perfections infinies. Je pardonnerai toujours du fond de rnon coeur à tous ceux qui pourraient m'offenser, comme je pardonne, dès à présent et sans réserve, à tous ceux qui peuvent m'avoir fait quelque offense: je vous prie, ô mon Dieu, de leur pardonner de même et de leur accorder votre grâce. J'éviterai avec soin de jamais offenser personne et, si j'avais ce malheur, je ne rougirai point de leur faire les réparations les plus satisfaisantes. Je serai toujours parfaitement soumis à tout ce qu'il plaira à votre divine providence d'ordonner de moi, et je recevrai toujours avec une résignation parfaite à votre suprêrne volonté tous les biens ou les maux qu'il vous plaira de m'envoyer. Je me préparerai à la mort, comme au jour où je devrai vous rendre compte de toutes mes actions, et je l'attendrai sans effroi, comme l'instant qui doit me délivrer de l'assujettissement au corps et me rejoindre à vous pour jamais. En un mot, ô mon souverain maître, j'emploierai ma vie à vous servir, à obéir à vos lois et à remplir mes devoirs: j'implore vos bénédictions sur ces résolutions, que je forme de tout mon coeur et avec un ferme propos de les exécuter, sachant par une triste expéience que, sans les secours de votre grâce, les plus fermes projets s'évanouissent, mais que vous ne la refusez jamais à ceux qui vous la demandent du coeur et avec humilité et ferveur.

J'implore les mêmes grâces, ô mon Dieu, sur ma chère maman, sur ma chère bienfaitrice, et sur mon cher père. Accordez-leur, Père des miséricordes, tous les secours dont ils ont besoin, pardonnez-leur tout le mal qu'ils ont fait, inspirez-leur le bien qu'ils doivent faire, et leur donnez la force de remplir et les devoirs de leur état et ceux que vous exigez d'eux. Souvenez-vous généralement de tous mes bienfaiteurs; faites retomber sur leurs têtes tous les biens qu'ils m'ont faits; accordez de même l'assistance de vos bénédictions divines à tous mes amis, à ma patrie et à tout le genre humain en général; souvenez-vous, ô mon Dieu, que vous êtes le Père commun de tous les hommes, et ayez pitié de nous tous dans la plénitude de vos miséricordes.

In this second prayer are developed two of the main themes which will occupy a prominent place in Rousseau's future outlook. They are: "the spiritual grandeur of the universe as God's handiwork and the need for personal virtue.[24] God is called here "King of nature" who exposes to our sight "the moving and magnificent spectacle of this vast universe." The concept of creation, *creatio ex nihilo*, is still affirmed here outright: "whatever magnificence prevails in the construction of this vast universe, I realize that to bring it out from nothingness in all its perfection, it required only one moment of Thy will." We also notice in this prayer a change from the plural pronoun "we" to the singular "I" and the possessive adjective "my," making it a very personal prayer. Guéhenno infers from this shift an indirect compensatory effect, namely that "his prayer . . . by the very fact of being confined himself alone, became magnificently eloquent."[25] It also has another effect. Following the recognition of God and His sovereignty, Jean-Jacques expresses his repentance in due form: admission of sin ("all the sins which I have committed, all the straying into which I have fallen . . . all the vices into which those weaknesses have led me. My conscience tells me how guilty I am"), confession ("I feel that all those pleasures that my passions set before me when I strayed from the path of wisdom are now worse than an illusion, and have turned into bitter and hateful memories"), remorse ("I am overwhelmed with regret for having made such poor use of a life and freedom which Thou hast granted me"), request of forgiveness ("pardon all the sins which I have committed till this day . . . deign to have pity on my weaknesses . . . accept my repentance, O my God") and resolution for the future ("Ashamed of my past faults, I make a firm resolution to make up for them by a conduct of rectitude and sobriety"). There follow more than thirty verbs in the future tense, marking his promise to do better toward God and toward fellow-man, such as: "Henceforth, I shall relate all my actions to Thee . . . I shall always keep Thy law in my heart . . . I shall love my neighbor as my-

---

[24] Cf.Grimsley, *Religious Writings*, p. 3.
[25] Cf. Guéhenno, I, 84.

self, I shall render service to him in everything that depends on me
. . . I shall resist temptation . . . I shall speak evil of no one," etc.
Guéhenno observes that, temporarily defeated by the act of living, he
had again become humble through suffering.[26] In this prayer also recurs Rousseau's belief that Divine mercy at least matches Divine omnipotence: "If Thy omnipotence is infinite, Thy Divine kindness is no
less than that." For Rousseau relies heavily on Divine goodness to
grant him pardon and peace of mind, so much so that in the last part
of this prayer, he concludes with a heartfelt appeal to the "Father of
mercies," a reminiscence, says Masson, of the manner in which the
Genevan pastor was accustomed to close the Sunday service. This expression also contains an involuntary but sure admission, Masson
concludes, that Calvinism, as the prayer shows, still lives in the heart
of the young Catholic of Les Charmettes.[27] To which we might add:
and surfaces particularly at times of stress and trial.

Of special significance to Jean-Jacques is the concept of God as an
all-seeing eye, at times also referred to as the Divine gaze or the Divine look: "I shall bear in mind that Thou art witness to all my deeds
and I shall endeavor to do nothing which is unworthy of Thy awesome presence." In the analysis of Grimsley: "Man is never allowed to
forget permanently that he is the *object* of the Divine gaze, that is, of a
gaze that is not without severity, especially for the soul conscious of
possible guilt[28] or the temptation of evil. God's presence, therefore, in
Rousseau's view, not only brings a sense of personal reality, but also
helps to confer a moral value on paradisiac existence."[29] The editors of
the Pléiade edition of Rousseau's works also take notice of the Divine
look element in this prayer and comment: "One sees appearing here
under a form by no means philosophical a theme which will be fundamental in the philosophy of Rousseau. Life under the gaze of God
is a commonplace idea of Christian devotion. However, in Rousseau,
it is this idea that will define my authentic *being* by opposing it to the

---

[26] Ibid.

[27] Cf. Masson, *La Religion de Jean-Jacques Rousseau*, I, 128.

[28] Cf. also Victor Hugo, *La Légende des siècles*, eye as a symbol for Divine presence in the poem "La Conscience," Bibliothèque de la Pléiade (Paris: Gallimard, 1950), pp. 25–26.

[29] Cf. Grimsley, *Religious Quest*, p. 109.

coming in sight that the gaze of the other defines. Consequently, God is gaze and, hence, such a God is very different from the one in deism."[30] While we have already expressed our view that Jean-Jacques was rather a theist than a deist, the only disagreement we have with the preceding is the remark that the Divine gaze is a "commonplace" idea. (idée "banale") of religious devotion. On the contrary, it seems to us, this idea is central to religion, as religion teaches man to consider himself always in the presence of God, which could well be a summary of the religious goal as it affects human conduct.[31]

While the concept of the Divine gaze, implying a personal God, is "very different from the one [God] in deism," the expression "engraved in my heart" as in "Thou hast engraved in the depth of my heart laws" is a favorite one of Rousseau and is associated with the idea of natural law.

Masson senses in this prayer not only a distinctive "Christian fervor" but also a piety that Jean-Jacques will not "know any longer," not hesitating about creation and about petitioning God as he will in his "Profession of Faith." Masson underscores that Jean-Jacques is praying here in the fullest sense of the word, for he is requesting help from on high, and pleads for Divine benedictions on himself and on those who are dear to him, to wit his dear late mother, his dear benefactress Mme de Warens, his dear father as well as to all his benefactors, his friends, his country and humanity in general. He does so with a deep humility and earnest repentance. Furthermore, Masson stresses, Jean-Jacques reveals an awareness of human misery, especially his own. All of these, according to Masson, will become purely theoretical during the mature years of Rousseau when he deals with God as with an equal. However, at this stage and in this prayer, we are witness to his love for retreat and solitude, a spirit of resignation, mortification of the senses and of the will, pardon for injury received,

---

[30] Cf. *O.C.* IV, 1764, note 1 to p. 1038.

[31] Cf. *Psalms*, xvi.8, p. 38: "I have set the Lord always before me," and footnote: "To have the consciousness of being always before Him must profoundly affect man's conduct in every circumstance." Incidentally, that verse from the Psalms is often affixed to the altar of synagogues and also constitutes the opening verse in the main authoritative compendium of Jewish law called *Shulchan Aruch*, followed by these words: "This is a leading principle in religion and in the upward strivings of the righteous who walk ever in the presence of God."

chastity—the entire Christian ideal seems to be in full bloom in this prayer.[32] We fail to see in this prayer mortification of the senses and of the will. Rousseau only asks God to "destroy in me all the *vices* into which those weaknesses have led me." He wants a redirection, a sublimation if you will, of his drives and impulses but not their destruction or elimination. We also fail to see his spirit of resignation. He says: "I feel that the only real pleasures are those we enjoy in practicing virtue and in carrying out the duties it prescribes." He wants God to help him act morally and asks not for passivity. Perhaps what he prays for can best be summed up in his words: "Henceforth, I shall relate all my actions to Thee," in other words to do what is right, what is moral. On the other hand, cardinal principles of Catholicism, such as reference to Jesus, the sacraments, the saints and the church are completely absent in this prayer even though it was composed in the Catholic period of Rousseau's. life—an absence which Rousseau admits, points to deism.

Thus, we see in these two early prayers elements of traditional religion side by side with deistic and some theistic elements (personal God, for example). It is these elements that will dominate in the prayers found in Rousseau's later writings.

---

[32]   Cf. Masson, *La Religion de Jean-Jacques Rousseau*, I, 124.

CHAPTER VI

Some Experiences
with Deistic Prayer

A. First Prayer—Rhetorical

In 1749, Rousseau's fame rested solely on his being a musician. He believed music to be his real vocation. His friend Diderot had also entrusted him with the writing of articles on music in the *Encyclopédie*.

Jean-Jacques became a writer by a fortuitous event: as he was walking from Paris to Vincennes to visit the imprisoned Diderot, he rested under a tree when he noticed in the October 1749 issue of the *Mercure de France* the subject of a prize essay announced by the Academy of Dijon. It read: *Si le rétablissement des sciences et des arts a contribué à épurer les moeurs.* He experienced then a quarter of an hour of ecstasy during which ideas flashed in his mind and he perceived with utmost clarity the development of the theme. This experience is referred to as the "illumination" of Vincennes. What happens to Rousseau, according to Masson's analysis, is that the doubt inherent in the question of the Academy ("*Si* le rétablissement…") imposes itself on him with great impact and becomes an opening, a fissure, through which all his long repressed feelings erupt and all his inner contradictions find their resolution. Now he perceives everything in a clear, lucid way. Rousseau called his experience a sudden "inspiration," an "illumination." Masson adds a key religious term: a "revelation" which is at the same time *un appel*, a calling, and notes: "What remounts into his consciousness is the unforgotten faith of his childhood and the pastoral Christianity with which he became bewitched at Les Charmettes."[1] Rousseau then reworded the Academy's ques-

---

[1]   Cf. Masson, *La Religion de Jean-Jacques Rousseau*, I, 165–66.

tion to read: "Si le *progrès* des sciences et des arts a contribué *à corrompre* ou à épurer les moeurs" and won the contest a year later.

In this *Discours sur les sciences et les arts*, Jean-Jacques claims that civilization has corrupted natural man and that the invention of printing which helped spread knowledge also helped spread corruption. Future generations, says Rousseau, will complain about it, will raise their hands to heaven and say with bitterness in their heart:

> "Alrnighty Cod, Thou who keepest all spirits in Thy hands, deliver us from the knowledge and the baleful arts of our forefathers and return to us ignorance, innocence and poverty, the only possessions that can make us happy and are precious in Thy sight."[2]

In a footnote, Professors Otis E. Fellows and Norman L. Torrey state: "Much of this paragraph is obviously pure rhetoric."[3] Now, rhetorical prayer has been resorted to by many other writers and, here, Rousseau does so, too, in his attempt to dramatize the ills that civilization harbors for future generations and against which he wants to protect mankind. The prayer is made more acceptable when it is addressed to Divinity, since the values Rousseau tries to preserve are for our good and are also precious to God, Jean-Jacques assures us. Some Christian or rather Catholic references are discernible in this prayer, like the happiness of the simple-minded and the extolling of poverty. To be sure, ignorance and poverty as ideals may also be found in "pagan-Socratic ignorance" or the poverty of certain Pythagorean and certain Stoic sects. Equally worth noticing in Rousseau are the general appellation "Almighty God" which is of Protestant usage and is employed here by the formally Catholic convert Rousseau, as well as the absence of any reference to Jesus—a characteristic of deistic prayer.

With this Discourse, Jean-Jacques became a writer *malgré lui*. While "success brings him back closer yet to Christianity,"[4] his decision to live in accord with his teachings and his persistence in being

---

[2] Cf. *O.C.* III, 28: "Dieu tout-puissant, toi qui tiens dans tes mains les esprits, délivre-nous des lumières et des funestes arts de nos pères, et rends-nous l'ignorance, l'innocence et la pauvreté, les seuls biens qui puissent faire notre bonheur et qui soient précieux devant toi."

[3] Otis E. Fellows and Norman L. Torrey, *The Age of Enlightenment* (New York: Appleton-Century-Crofts, 1942), p. 493.

[4] Cf. Masson, *La Religion de Jean-Jacques Rousseau*, I, 291.

out of tune with the main currents of the century will soon enough lead to his break with the *philosophes*.

B. Prayer Without Words—Speechless Adoration

An unfinished religious allegory believed to have been composed during the 1750's (before his "Profession of Faith") was given no title by the author himself but G. Streckeisen-Moultou first published it in 1861 as *Fiction ou Morceau allégorique sur la révélation*.

In a chapter entitled "'Professions de foi' avant la 'profession du vicaire,'" Masson qualifies this allegory as a "philosophical-religious meditation" which was improperly called *Allégorie sur la révélation* and adds that he finds here, as in the *Profession*, a dual religious problem: first the problem of the world and of life which finds its solution in the concept of God and then the problem of revelation. The first problem is dealt with directly when the *philosophe*, like the Vicar, meditates on the universe while contemplating the beauty of nature. Both face the same questions about the origin of the universe, of thought in material, physical beings and the relationship between matter and movement. The Vicar, however, has an advantage: his intellectual equipment enables him to resolve problems through reason and then, if need be, to have recourse to feeling. On the other hand, the thinker who will fall asleep and become a dreamer is less mature intellectually and he would fail to grasp the meaning of what he sees were it not for celestial favor or something akin to grace which rewards him for his sincere love of truth and his intellectual humility. Then, in a type of inner illumination, he grasps the meaning of the performance of the cosmic machine and of the universal and consoling explanation that is God and this first meditation ends up in prayer to the common Father of all mankind.[5] The prayer of speechless adoration reads:

> In the presence of these great and bewitching lights [ideas], his soul, overcome by admiration, and rising so to speak to the level of the object that occupied it, felt itself imbued with a lively and delicious sensation: a spark of this Divine fire that it had noted seemed to give it a new life; enraptured

---

[5]   Cf. Masson, *La Religion de Jean-Jacques Rousseau*, II, 50–51.

by respect, gratitude and zeal, he rises hurriedly; then, raising his eyes and his hands toward heaven and bowing down afterwards with face toward the earth, his heart and his lips addressed to the Divine Being the first and perhaps the purest homage that He ever received from a mortal.[6]

The thinker adores the majesty and power of the Creator in silence. Adoration, according to the Encyclopaedia Britannica, is "generally considered the most noble form of prayer, a kind of prostration of the whole being before God.... To express his adoration, man often falls to the ground and prostrates himself. The feeling of submissive reverence also is expressed by body movements: raising the hands...deep bowing of the body...prostration...to the ground. The gesture often is accompanied by cries of fear, amazement or joy."[7] This last point of accompanying cry will be apparent in the next two prayers. Before proceeding further, let us point out that the thinker in this prayer raised himself to the conception of a transcendental God, which is another characteristic of deistic prayer. Adoration then takes on its fullest meaning in the presence of the transcendental God and the utmost expression of adoration is utter silence. Curiously though not surprisingly to us, Maimonides, referring to an ideal world, also considers silence as the ultimate praise of God. He finds Biblical sanction for this concept in the book of Psalms (lxv.2) which says: "Silence[8] is praise to Thee" and he adds: "...it is...more becoming to be silent and to be content with intellectual reflection [in modern terms: adoration, contemplation, meditation], as has been recommended by

---

[6]   Cf. *O.C.* IV, 1047–48. See also Grimsley, *Religious Writings*, p. 84: "A ces grandes et ravissantes lumières [idées], son âme, saisie d'admiration et s'élevant pour ainsi dire au niveau de l'objet qui l'occupait, se sentit pénétrée d'une sensation vive et délicieuse: une étincelle de ce feu divin qu'elle avait aperçue semblait lui donner une nouvelle vie; transporté de respect, de reconnaissance et de zèle, il se lève précipitamment; puis, élevant les yeux et les mains vers le ciel et s'inclinant ensuite la face contre terre, son coeur et sa bouche adressèrent à l'Etre divin le premier et peut-être le plus pur hommage qu'il ait jamais reçu des mortels."

[7]   [Rev.] A[dalbert] G. Ha[mman], *The New Encyclopaedia Britannica-Macropaedia*, 1974, XIV, 950.

[8]   Most English translations of the Psalms take the word "doomiyah" to mean waiting and, therefore., render the verse as: "Praise waiteth for Thee, O God." However, in most other places of the Bible, this root denotes silence and most Hebrew commentators (like Rashi, the commentator *par excellence*) understand "doomiyah" in this verse, too, as meaning silence. So does Maimonides.

men of the highest culture [i.e., wise men who recommended silent praise of God] in the words [of David]: 'Commune with your own heart upon your bed, *and be still*'" (Psalms iv. 5).[9] Indeed, prayer is fundamentally an inner act of the heart.

C. The Overflowing Heart—Prayer as Ecstatic Cry

"I began to live only on April 9, 1756" (date of his installation at L'Ermitage), Jean-Jacques wrote on January 26, 1762 in his third letter to M. de Malesherbes. In it, says Grimsley, Jean-Jacques gave a particularly eloquent account of his inner life and of his reactions to nature with which he always associated religion. His description of his infinite longing for nature constitutes an added dimension to his religious experience.[10] We spoke before of the attitude of speechless adoration which Rousseau adopted toward nature. Here, the adoration culminates in an ecstatic cry to God:

> Soon, from the surface of the earth, I raised my ideas toward all the creatures of nature, to the universal system of matter, to the incomprehensible Being who embraces everything. Then, with my mind lost in this immensity, I did not think, I did not reason, I did not philosophize: with a kind of sensuousness, I felt overwhelmed by the weight of this universe, I abandoned myself with rapture to the confusion of these great ideas, I loved to lose myself in imagination in space; my heart, confined within the limits of our being, found itself there pinched for room. I felt stifled in the universe, I should have liked to soar up into the infinite. Had I unravelled all the mysteries of nature, my situation would have been, I think, less delightful than this intoxicating ecstasy to which my spirit abandoned itself without reserve and which, in the excitement of my raptures, made me cry out sometimes: "O great Being! O great Being!" unable to say or think anything more.[11]

---

[9] Moses Maimonides, *Guide of the Perplexed*, translated and annotated by M. Friedlander (New York: Hebrew Publishing Co., n.d.), Part I, chap. 59, p. 216.

[10] Cf. Grimsley, *Religious Writings*, p. 101.

[11] Cf. *A M. de Malesherbes* (third letter), 1762, *O.C.* I, 1141: "Bientôt de la surface de la terre, j'élevais mes idées à tous les êtres de la nature, au système universel des choses, à l'Etre incompréhensible qui embrasse tout. Alors, l'esprit perdu dans cette immensité, je ne pensais pas, je ne raisonnais pas, je ne philosophais pas: je me sentais, avec une sorte de volupté, accablé du poids de cet univers, je me li-

We have here, according to Masson, "the abandonment to the Great Being and the swooning ecstasy amidst Divine nature."[12] The experience is overwhelming and of a deep cosmic mysticism. The Encyclopaedia Britannica puts it this way: "In the presence of the mystery of the Divine, man often discovers that he can only stammer or that his speech often falters.... Religious language, like silence, thus expresses the distance and inadequacy of man in relation to the Divine mystery."[13] And that distance, as we know, is emphasized by deism.

D. Prayer as Silent Wonder

In a letter addressed to the Genevan minister Jacob Vernes on February 18, 1758, Jean-Jacques wrote: "I am a religious man, my friend, and it is well for me that it is so; I do not believe that anyone in the world needs religion as much as I do."[14] For him, the main evidence of the existence of God was, as we know, that he felt His presence and also felt a need for God. In his keen analysis of Rousseau's philosophy, Harald Höffding tells us that, at its peak, this need reaches a superabundance that our finite world is incapable of containing and, therefore, Rousseau feels stifled in the universe. Only when he is in open nature, does this feeling stir in him and he feels at one with nature in all that lives. Then, Höffding notes, "in extreme joy

---

vrais avec ravissement à la confusion de ces grandes idées, j'aimais à me perdre en imagination dans l'espace; mon coeur reserré dans les bornes des êtres s'y trouvait trop à l'étroit, j'étouffais dans l'univers, j'aurais voulu m'élancer dans l'infini. Je crois que, si j'eusse dévoilé tous les mystères de la nature, je me serais senti dans une situation moins délicieuse que cette étourdissante extase, à laquelle mon esprit se livrait sans retenue, et qui, dans l'agitation de mes transports, me faisait écrire quelquefois: O grand Etre! ô grand Etre! sans pouvoir dire ni penser rien de plus."

[12] Cf. Masson, *La Religion de Jean-Jacques Rousseau*, II, 30.

[13] Cf. [Rev.] A[dalbert] G. Ha[mman], *The New Encyclopaedia Britannica*, 1974; XIV, 949.

[14] *Correspondance générale de Jean-Jacques Rousseau*, collationnée par Théophile Dufour (Paris: Armand Colin. 1925), vol. III, letter no. 474, pp. 286–87: "J'ai de la religion, mon ami, et bien m'en prend; je ne crois pas qu'homme du monde en ait autant besoin que moi."

and wonder at life, his thoughts roamed from object to object until at last they joined the great all, eternity, by which he felt himself surrounded. Every conception, every idea proved insufficient, and only an explosion of feeling could relieve the emotional state. Rousseau's religious emotion at its height was silent wonder."[15]

The mute admiration bursting out in an ecstatic cry which tries to express the inexpressible silent wonder is recorded in the twelfth book of the *Confessions*. Rousseau writes:

> I can think of no worthier homage to the Divinity than the mute admiration which is aroused by the contemplation of His works, and does not find expression in outward acts.... In my room, my prayers are not so frequent or so fervent; but, at the sight of a beautiful landscape, I feel myself moved without knowing why. I remember reading of a wise bishop who, during a visit to his diocese, came upon an old woman who, by way of prayer, could say nothing but "Oh!" "Good mother," said the bishop, "continue to pray in this manner: your prayer is better than ours." This better prayer is also mine.[16]

Let us note that the last sentence is Rousseau's own conclusion from that story. One exclamation by a person who is overwhelmed by the immeasurable mystery of God is, in Rousseau's definition, equal if not superior to a most eloquent prayer.

E. Hypothetical Prayer

Jean-Jacques wrote his *Letter on Providence* on August 18, 1756 as a reply to Voltaire's *Poem on the Disaster of Lisbon* which he had received from its author the preceding June. In it, Rousseau refutes Voltaire's

---

[15]   Harald Höffding, *Jean-Jacques Rousseau and His Philosophy* (New Haven: Yale University Press, 1930), translated from the second Danish edition by William Richards and Leo E. Saidla, p. 120.

[16]   Cf. *Les Confessions*, O.C., vol. I, Book 12, p. 642: "Je ne trouve point de plus digne hommage à la Divinité que cette admiration muette qu'excite la contemplation de ses oeuvres, et qui ne s'exprime point par des actes développés....Dans ma chambre, je prie plus rarement et plus sèchement: mais à l'aspect d'un beau paysage, je me sens ému sans pouvoir dire de quoi. J'ai lu qu'un sage évêque, dans la visite de son diocèse, trouva une vieille femme qui, pour toute prière, ne savait dire que'O!' Il lui dit: 'Bonne mère, continuez de prier toujours ainsi; votre prière vaut mieux que les nôtres.' Cette meilleure prière est aussi la mienne."

pessimism following the tragic earthquake in Lisbon, reasserts his own consoling belief in a general, benevolent Providence and in the survival of the soul and blames man's cupidity for the extent of the casualties and damages Lisbon suffered.

In this letter, too, Rousseau affirms his belief in the superiority of morality over dogma (a deistic creed) in view of which the unbelieving man who acts in good faith will be granted eternal bliss by Providence. It is in this context that we find Rousseau's hypothetical prayer, prayer in the sense that it involves communication with God:

> "...I would prefer to be able to say to God, *I did, without thinking of Thee, the good which is pleasing to Thee, and my heart followed Thy will without knowing it,* than to say to Him, as I will have to do one day: *Alas! I loved Thee and I have not ceased to offend Thee, I have known Thee and did nothing to please Thee.*"[17]

The indifference to dogma and the emphasis on good deeds (social morality) as well as general optimism are deistic elements clearly apparent in this prayer. So is the reliance on the supremacy of Divine goodness over Divine omnipotence and an assumption of universal agreement on what constitutes a good deed. However, it is striking that in a letter which so forcefully presents the concept of a general, impersonal Providence, Jean-Jacques should visualize himself in future, personal judgment before God, something which rather belongs to revealed religion which posits belief in a personal God. What comes through here, apparently, is his early religious upbringing and attitude toward God to which he reverts probably unconsciously. We

---

[17]   Cf. *Letter to Voltaire on Providence, O.C.* IV, 1078: "...j'aimerais mieux pouvoir dire à Dieu, *J'ai fait, sans songer à toi, le bien qui t'est agréable, et mon coeur suivait ta volonté sans la connaître,* que de lui dire, comme il faudra que je fasse un jour: *Hélas! je t'aimais et n'ai cessé de t'offenser, je t'ai connu et n'ai rien fait pour te plaire.*"

know that in 1754, two years before writing this letter, Jean-Jacques had returned to being a citizen of Geneva and reaccepted his Calvinist faith formally, for civic reasons, true enough, but this return also seems to have awakened in him elements of his early religiosity.

CHAPTER VII

Prayer and its Definition in *La Nouvelle Héloïse*

La Nouvelle Héloïse was published in 1761. Its popularity can be gauged by the fact that seventy editions of the book had appeared by the year 1800.[1] To a century dominated by rationalism, Jean-Jacques revealed the rights of the heart, of emotional life, and the reading public took to it thirstily. It is a novel in epistolary form between Julie d'Etange and Saint-Preux, her tutor; but other characters exchange letters with one another and with the two principal personages as well. It parallels in part Rousseau's own life and dreams, in particular his actual and potential relationship with Sophie d'Houdetot, and the letters reflect in large measure his personal views. Saint-Preux is generally taken to be his spokesman but the *dédoublement* that Rousseau later made of himself into (the Calvinist, serious-minded) Rousseau and (the tender, soft-hearted) Jean-Jacques would tend to make us think that Julie, too, may represent ideas close to him—in our context, ideas about prayer.

The novel depicts two crises: one at the time of Julie's wedding to M. de Wolmar and the other prior to her premature death as a result of illness contracted while saving her son from drowning. Prayers appear on both occasions and assume overriding importance as Jean-Jacques decides to expand the book and the role of religion in it. In-between, too, are present discussions on the function of prayer. In this Chapter, we shall, therefore, analyze all these in the order in which they appear in the novel.

---

[1]   Daniel Mornet, *Civilisation française*, Nov.-Dec. 1919, quoted by Albert Schinz in his *Vie et oeuvres de Jean-Jacques Rousseau* (Boston, New York, Chicago: D.C. Heath, 1921), p. 207.

A. Prayer as Homage to God

When Julie reluctantly accedes to the demand of her father that she marry an old friend of his, M. de Wolmar, she and Saint-Preux plan on deceiving him and continue their relationship clandestinely. In the words of Saint-Preux: "Why should we alone try to behave more chastely than the rest of humanity and, with childish simplicity, observe illusory virtues that everyone talks about but nobody practices? Can we hope to be better moralists than the swarms of scholars in London and Paris who all mock at conjugal fidelity and look upon adultery as a game?…Can a husband suffer through an act of infidelity of which he knows nothing?"[2]

Suddenly, there is a turn-about and it happens during the marriage ceremony at the Protestant Temple where Julie undergoes a complete transformation. Some critics consider her experience "an act of renovation," a sudden "inner revolution," a "reorientation of her emotions."[3] Others consider it "a brusque illumination which Rousseau presents to us as Divine grace."[4] Daniel Mornet sees in it a "Divine intervention…for God takes part in it."[5] Whatever its nature, we agree with Mornet that the experience at the marriage ceremony is the center of the novel: "No doubt, the marriage scene of Julie where this Divine intervention blazes forth is the center of the novel; or rather what the deliberate will of Rousseau wanted to put into the center….The turning point of the novel which directs it toward duty and not toward pleasure is in the Temple, at the very moment when the marriage ceremony ceases to be a human ceremony to call forth the Divine presence.[6]

In a long letter to Saint-Preux in which she reviews her life from the time she met him in a kind of *examen de conscience*, Julie describes

---

[2]   Cf. *La Nouvelle Héloïse*, Part 3, Letter XVI, *O.C.* II, 337. See also. Guéhenno, I, 366–67.

[3]   F.C. Green, *Jean-Jacques Rousseau—A Critical Study of his Life and Writings* (Cambridge: Cambridge University Press, 1955, p. 196.

[4]   Robert Mauzi, "La Conversion de Julie dans *Le Nouvelle Héloïse*"in *Société Jean-Jacques Rousseau annales* (Genève: A Jullien, 1959/62), XXXV, 33.

[5]   *"La Nouvelle Héloïse"* de Jean-Jacques Rousseau, étude et analyse par Daniel Mornet (Paris: Editions Mellottée, 1929), p. 168.

[6]   Ibid.

in detail her experience during the marriage ceremony. She had let herself be led to the Temple as an "impure victim which sullies the very ceremony in which it is about to be sacrificed." However, once inside the Temple, she is overcome by a kind of emotion she had never felt before. The atmosphere of holiness permeating the house of worship, the dim light and the respectful silence of the assembled, all of these impress her deeply. Moreover, in the pastor's recitation of the marriage liturgy, she seems to hear the voice of God. Then, with a sense of awe, she feels that the "all-seeing eye"—a favorite key word and key concept of Rousseau—is looking at her and scrutinizing her innermost thoughts. Something happens suddenly to her inner self which effects a change in her feelings and her thoughts. She becomes a new person. The disorder in her soul is stilled and its passions now function "according to the law of duty and nature." There is harmony now between her heart and her will and she fully and sincerely pronounces her marriage vows. The marriage bond is now seen as a new state capable of purifying her soul and restoring it to its pristine essence. She feels, indeed, like a new person "freshly emerged from the hands of Nature." Following the ceremony, and in order to test the quality of her conversion, Julie asks for an hour of solitude and self-contemplation. She then discovers to her great joy that, although she still loves Saint-Preux, the love has changed its nature. She also discovers that she can think of Saint-Preux with a calm conscience and no disturbance, no sensual desire, no embarrassment whatever. Aware of this new plane she has reached, she thinks with horror about the road of vice she might have taken, were it not for God's merciful intervention which saved her from a fatal step on the brink of the abyss. A stylistic device reflects the emotional intensity of her gratitude for Divine protection. Julie begins five sentences in this letter with the interrogative pronoun ."who" ("qui"): "Who has shielded me from so natural a consequence of my first mistake? Who has held me back…? Who has preserved my reputation…? Who has placed me under the protection of so virtuous a spouse…? Who, in short, enables me still to aspire to the title of a respectable wife…?"[7] This repetition of "who" ("qui") accentuates her indebtedness to the benefactor

---

[7]   Cf. Letter XVIII, Part 3, *O.C.* II, 356.

whom she identifies as "the helping hand" and to whom now, in a crescendo of fervor, she pays a prayerful homage:

> "Eternal Providence who dost make the insect crawl and the heavens revolve, Thou art watchful over the least of all Thy works! Thou hast recalled me to that virtue which I was born to revere; deign, therefore, to receive from a heart purified by Thy goodness that homage which Thou alone hast rendered worthy of Thy acceptance."[8]

We notice in this prayer a clear affirmation of the belief in a personal Providence that watches over all His creatures and to whom Julie is most grateful for her regeneration and rebirth. This is in total opposition to the deistic belief in a general, impersonal Providence. What does this mean in terms of Rousseau's deism and the assumed deistic nature of his prayers? Two possibilities emerge. One is that whenever a deeply emotional situation arises that impels him to introduce prayer, the rational concept of a non-personal Deity gives way, disappears, and the content of the prayer expresses or implies a belief in an individual Providence. When emotion is strong enough, the resulting prayer apparently assumes the traditional character of direct appeal to a personal Deity that is close to man. In this prayer, following Julie's marriage, the overwhelming experiences of this day of days in her life certainly lead to a highly emotional state and her feelings are poured into a traditional prayer to a Deity that listens and responds. Of course, we cannot tell if Jean-Jacques himself would have prayed this way under similar circumstances or he merely found that Julie's character demanded it. A second possibility is that Rousseau, in today's meaning of the terms, is a theist rather than a deist, a position that commends itself more and more as we proceed in our study. We have indicated at the beginning of this study that in the eighteenth century the designations of theist and deist were used interchangeably—as in Voltaire's *Philosophical Dictionary* in which there is an entry for Théiste but none for Déiste. Similarly, Diderot, in his translation into French of the works of the noted English deist, the

---

8   Ibid., p. 356: "Providence éternelle, qui fais ramper l'insecte et rouler les cieux, tu veilles sur la moindre de tes oeuvres! Tu me rappelles au bien que tu m'as fait aimer; daigne accepter d'un coeur épuré par tes soins l'hommage que toi seule rends digne de t'être offert."

Earl of Shaftesbury, often renders "deism" as théisme.[9] However, as the philosophy of religion has been pursued with greater attention, more defined and exact connotations were given these terms. In the nineteenth and twentieth centuries, we are informed, "the word deism was used theologically in contradistinction to theism, the belief in an immanent God who actively intervenes in the affairs of men. In this sense, deism was represented as the view of those who reduced the role of God to a mere act of creation in accordance with rational laws discoverable by man and held that, after the original act, God virtually withdrew and refrained from interfering in the processes of nature and the ways of man. "[10] According to this definition, Rousseau would be a theist, at least in those instances where he is impelled to compose intensely emotional prayers. While direct address to God and the absence of an intermediary and of other elements characteristic of Christianity are part of deism, they do conform to theism as well.

B. Prayer for Aid in Overcoming Possible Future Moral Weakness

Having paid homage to Providence, Julie becomes fully aware of the danger she had been delivered from and of the state of "honor" and "security" she has been restored to. Whereupon, in a manner reminiscent of submissive reverence in adoration prayer,[11] Julie bows to the ground, raises her supplicating hands heavenwards and prays for Divine assistance:

> I want, said I, the good that Thou wantest and of which Thou alone art the source. I want to love the spouse that Thou hast given to me. I want to be faithful because it is the chief duty which unites private families and society in general. I want to be chaste because it is the parent virtue which nourishes all the others. I want everything relative to the order of nature which Thou hast established and to the dictates of reason which I derive

---

[9] [Prof.] F[rank] E[dward] M[anuel], The *New Encyclopaedia Britannica*, 1974, V, 562.

[10] Ibid.

[11] Cf. [Rev.] A[dalbert] G. Ha[mman], *The New Encyclopaedia Britannica*, 1974, XIV, on adoration, 950.

from Thee. I entrust my heart to Thy protection and my desires to Thy guidance. Render all my actions conformable to my steadfast will, which is ever Thine, and never more permit momentary error to triumph over the settled choice of my life.[12]

Julie explicitly calls the above "prayer" and adds that, after this brief prayer, she felt strengthened in her resolutions.

In the previous prayer of homage, it was the heart that found itself. Now, Julie prays that her future actions may conform to her present will. "I want" ("Je veux"), repeated four times, emphasizes her determination to live according to the rules of nature and reason.

Describing her sentiments during the marriage ceremony, Julie had said that the "disorder of [her] affections" was corrected according to the law "of duty and nature." In this prayer, too, she asks for God's help to live according to the "order of nature" and the "dictates (or rules) of reason." The "order of nature" is important to Rousseau and to Julie, for man can obtain special satisfaction when he can identify himself with the universal system.[13] Robert Mauzi goes even further and ascribes what Julie thinks as the intervention of grace in her change as being in reality "a profoundly Rousseauistic idea": "the identity of nature with grace."[14] Concerning the place of reason in Rousseau's thought, it is the "Divine torch ("flambeau divin") which God has given man for his guidance.[15] It is, therefore, consistent with

---

[12] Cf. *La Nouvelle Héloïse*, Part 3, Letter XVIII, *O.C.* II, 356–57: "Je veux, lui dis-je, le bien que tu veux, et dont toi seul es la source. Je veux aimer l'époux que tu m'as donné. Je veux être fidèle, parce que c'est le premier devoir qui lie la famille et toute la société. Je veux être chaste, parce que c'est la première vertu qui nourrit toutes les autres. Je veux tout ce qui se rapporte à l'ordre de la nature que tu as établi, et aux règles de la raison que je tiens de toi. Je remets mon coeur sous ta garde et mes désirs en ta main. Rends toutes mes actions conformes à ma volonté constante qui est la tienne, et ne permets plus que l'erreur d'un moment l'emporte sur le choix de toute ma vie." See also partial translation in *French Thought in the Eighteenth Century*, "Jean-Jacques Rousseau" by Romain Rolland (New York: David McKay, 1953), p. 94.

[13] Cf. Grimsley, Religious Quest, p. 44.

[14] Cf. Robert Mauzi, p. 32.

[15] Cf. Letter XVIII, Part 3, *O.C.* II, 362. See also Grimsley, *Religious Quest*, p. 50, note on the distinction made by R. Derathé between psychological and metaphysical aspects of Rousseau's discussion of reason: in *Emile*, he is interested primarily in

Rousseau's outlook to pray for "everything" ("tout") that relates to the "order of nature" and the "dictates (or rules) of reason" that we "derive from God" ("que je tiens de toi"). Grimsley explains this sentence of Julie's prayer in the following manner: "Reason is important as a means of making us aware of the truth of our being; it also enables us to discern the total pattern of our existence within the universal order. All rational truths will ultimately conform with the principle of order, whereas prejudice and arbitrary power seek to violate it. Significantly enough, when Julie, at the time of her marriage, offers a prayer to God, she affirms: 'I want everything relative to the order of nature which Thou hast established and to the dictates of reason which I derive from Thee.'"[16]

In a later section of the novel, there will be a discussion on prayers of request as opposed to prayers of adoration. We believe it worthy to be noted a finding by Henri Gouhier to the effect that, practically, in this prayer following the marriage ceremony, Julie reconciles both, for she says: "Render all my actions conformable to my steadfast will which is ever Thine."[17]

Discussing later the prayer of request (petition), Saint-Preux will say: "It is not He who changes us; it is we who change ourselves in lifting ourselves up toward Him."[18] Masson who finds Julie's prayers to be "more satisfied than entreating and humbled," concludes, therefore, that if Julie does not subscribe theoretically to Saint-Preux's definition, she does so practically.[19] It appears to us that perhaps it is so in the sentence beginning with "I want" ("je veux") in which Julie expresses her just-acquired will to be loyal to her spouse. However, concerning the future, she is somewhat apprehensive about her ability to act in accordance with this, her present will, and not deviate from it, and for that she does solicit Divine help by saying that she entrusts her heart and her desires in God's hands ("I entrust my heart to

---

its role in the development of human personality, while elsewhere he is concerned with its power to illuminate the structure ("order") of reality as a whole.

[16] Cf. Grimsley, *Religious Quest*, p. 48.

[17] Henri Gouhier, *Les Méditations métaphysiques de J.-J. Rousseau* (Paris: J. Vrin, 1970), p. 123, note 30.

[18] Cf. *La Nouvelle Héloïse*, Part 6, Letter VII, O.C. II, 684: "Ce n'est pas lui qui nous change; c'est nous qui changeons en nous élevant à lui."

[19] Cf. Masson, *La Religion de Jean-Jacques Rousseau*, II, 76.

Thy protection.... Render all my actions conformable...and never more permit....") and asks Him for help.

In reflecting on Julie's petition in the last sentences of this prayer, we find that its subject depends on the interpretation we give to her experience during the marriage ceremony. Julie thinks that what she experienced was a state of grace which restored her to harmony with God's will. However, she is apprehensive about the future constancy of her newly recovered "steadfast will" and she is clearly worried about her ability to make her future actions conform with her present will. Therefore, she is petitioning God to keep her in that state of grace in the future, too, so that she may never falter.

Robert Mauzi, on the other hand, first sums up what occurred during the marriage ceremony: "Rousseau explains to us that Julie recovers during the ceremony her state of natural innocence, of original purity, but that happens under the impact of an intervention, of an illumination by grace." Then, he adds his own interpretation: "Here makes its appearance this profoundly Rousseauistic idea of the identity of nature with grace.[20] Later, he identifies the experience in a similar way: "Her conversion...is, therefore,...the triumph...of genuine nature."[21] In this light, Julie's prayer would be that this true nature remain dominant, so that her future deeds conform to her present "steadfast will" achieved as a result of that return to nature. This view of grace being identical with nature is also by implication a denial of the doctrine of original sin—and a deistic teaching. Julie's writing toward the end of the letter that "in this upheaval we sometimes resume our primitive character and become like a new being recently formed by the hands of nature,"[22] also points to a denial of the concept of original sin.

René Pomeau gives us the psychological approach. He begins with the statement that the marriage ceremony restores Julie to her own self. Then, he asks whether that was really caused by the supernatural intervention of grace. His answer is in the negative. He feels

---

[20]   Cf. Mauzi, p. 32.

[21]   Ibid., p. 33.

[22]   Cf. Letter XVIII, Part 3, O.C. II, 364: "dans ce bouleversement général on reprend quelquefois son caractère primitif et l'on devient comme un nouvel être sorti récemment des mains de la nature."

that only Julie thinks it was grace and that Rousseau has left to her the responsibility for this interpretation, while he slips under her pen words which cast light on the psychology of conversion. Thus, she discovers that by deciding to adhere to her marriage vows with integrity, she finds "happiness, order and peace," and that the "disorder of her affections" is rectified in accordance with the law of duty and nature. Moreover, once reinstated to a position of "honor and security," Julie senses in herself "a flood of pure joy." Pomeau then concludes by saying: "Marriage has restored her into the Divine plan, under the double safeguard of Wolmar and of Providence.... A happy fervor of devotion then fills her soul; she relishes at length the sweet blissfulness of feeling herself placed in a system where everything is fine."[23] To which we wish to add: and wants to maintain herself in that order, which is why she prays for future protection to let her remain in the state she has felicitously attained on that day. In the psychological explanation, too, original sin is absent.

Personally, we are inclined to view the "steadfast will" as expressing the belief that deep down, in the innermost core of our being, we want what God wants, deep down our will and God's will are identical. The problem is our ability to act according to our deeper will. For that, Julie prays to God to enable her to overcome weakness or momentary desires which may go counter to the "steadfast will" which she asserts to be at one with God's will. Now, whichever interpretation we may favor, the fact remains that Julie seeks strength and inspiration through prayer. For, as George R. Havens notes, prayer "overcomes the moral weakness of which Julie, like Jean-Jacques himself, is only too conscious."[24] We wish to make only a slight correction: prayer does not by itself "overcome" moral weakness, but, in prayer, Julie asks for Divine help, which help will enable her to overcome moral weakness. Her present sense of euphoria and victory is due to faith and trust, that help has come and will come again when needed.

---

[23]   J.-J. Rousseau, Julie *ou La Nouvelle Héloïse* (Paris: Garnier, 1960), introduction par René Pomeau, pp. xxxvi-xxxvii and note 1 on p. xxxvii.

[24]   Cf. *The Age of Ideas*, p. 270.

C. Julie's Discovery of Real Prayer, Meant and Felt Innerly

In the same long letter in which Julie describes the metamorphosis she underwent during the marriage ceremony, she speaks of her subsequent praying "with true zeal" and draws the conclusion that henceforth she will find the strength to resist temptation—in prayer. Though she had never been quite without religion, still what she had taken for religion was only the external manifestation of it and not the deeply-felt internal attuning of the heart to it. There was also a dichotomy between her participation in public worship and her inability to apply religion in practical ways to life. The same holds true with regards to the prayers which were to her only words repeated mechanically, not deeply-felt, not even identified with, and which did not touch her heart or influence her life. Having now found a source of strength in prayer, she recommends to Saint-Preux to find security himself in prayer invested with zeal and feeling: "Adore the Supreme Being, my worthy and prudent friend; with one puff of breath you will be able to dissipate those chimeras of reason which have only a futile appearance and which fly like so many shadows before immutable truth."[25] As we notice, Julie follows up her advice about praying with a scathing attack on the "vain sophisms of reason which has nothing to support it but itself" and which the *philosophes*, "worthy advocates of crime," use to excuse adultery. In the words of Julie: "But look, please, how they absolve adultery committed in secret! It is because, they say, no harm results from it, not even to the husband who does not know about it. As if they could be sure that he will never find out; as if one could justify perjury and infidelity by their not hurting anyone; as if the harm which a crime causes to those who commit it is not sufficient reason to abhor it. What! Is it not evil to be faithless, to annihilate as much as one can the power of the oath and of the most inviolable contract? Does it do no harm to force oneself to become a cheat and a liar?…. Does it not do any harm to be in a state which always produces a thousand other crimes? Even

---

25   Cf. Letter XVIII, Part 3, *O.C.* 11, 358: "Adorez l'Etre Eternel, mon digne et sage ami; d'un souffle vous détruirez ces fantômes de raison qui n'ont qu'une vaine apparence, et fuient comme une ombre devant l'immuable vérité."

something good which led to so many evils would thereby itself become evil too."[26] Furthermore, says Julie, the very presumption that the adultery was indeed completely secret cannot stand up if those *philosophes* believe in the existence of God and in the immortality of the soul since He is witness of everything in the world. But even on the purely human level, the claim that adultery which remains secret does not hurt anyone is unfounded.[27] And Julie (i.e. Rousseau) goes on to elaborate on the ravages of adultery,[28] of which she and Saint-Preux had almost been the victims. Here, too, Jean-Jacques begins the attack on the *philosophes* of his time, though they had all along treated him with special regard. Henceforth, he will remain a loner, pursuing his own way and using the literary and intellectual weapons of the *philosophes* to disprove them.

Speaking of the three phases of *La Nouvelle Héloïse*, Philippe Van Tieghem says that the novel "began by being the idyllic and sensual dream of spring, then became the dream of a happy life founded on a paradoxical situation, and ended up on moral and philosophical views on the secret of happiness and on true religion."[29] It is also in the sixth and last part of the book that we find an extensive epistolary discussion on prayer between Julie and Saint-Preux, particularly on petitionary prayer.

---

[26] Ibid., p. 359: "Mais voyez, je vous prie, comment ils disculpent un adultère se-cret! C'est, disent-ils, qu'il n'en résulte aucun mal, pas même pour l'époux qui l'ignore. Comme s'ils pouvaient être sûrs qu'il l'ignorera toujours; comme s'il suffisait pour autoriser le parjure et l'infidélité qu'ils ne nuisissent pas à autrui; comme si ce n'était pas assez pour abhorrer le crime du mal qu'il fait à ceux qui le commettent. Quoi donc! ce n'est pas un mal de manquer de foi, d'anéantir au-tant qu'il est en soi la force du serment et des contrats les plus inviolables? Ce n'est pas un mal de se forcer soi-même à devenir fourbe et menteur?…. Ce n'est pas un mal qu'un état dont mille autres crimes sont toujours le fruit? Un bien qui produirait tant de maux serait par cela seul un mal lui-même."

[27] Ibid., p. 360.

[28] Cf. "La Nouvelle Héloïse" de J.-J. Rousseau, étude et analyse par Daniel Mornet who sums it up thus on p. 176: "Etre adultère, c'est trahir un serment, offenser Dieu, introduire dans la famille des enfants d'un sang étranger, se condamner au mensonge, susciter la discorde et les crimes."

[29] Philippe Van Tieghem, *"La Nouvelle Héloïse" de J.-J. Rousseau* (Paris: Nizet, 1956), pp. 64–65.

D. Julie's Defense of Prayer and Some of Her Conceptions of It

The correspondence between Julie and Saint-Preux had been interrupted after the farewell ("adieu") of Julie in the twentieth letter of the third part of the book and resumed only with the sixth letter of the sixth and last part of the book. We know that the extension of the novel was an afterthought of Rousseau. Saint-Preux, too, will tell us that seven years[30] have elapsed since their last correspondence. Now, in the sixth part of the book, we unexpectedly find a discussion on the function of prayer in letters six, seven and eight. They contain respectively Julie's defense of her conception of prayer, Saint-Preux's conception and finally Julie's again. We may also keep in mind that this dialogue on prayer may well represent just Rousseau discoursing with himself.

It is Julie who initiates the dialogue in the book by referring to previously expressed views on the subject of prayer by Saint-Preux. Those views, however, do not appear in the book in any of the previous letters by Saint-Preux. We are then left to conjecture that either a letter has been lost or that the views were expressed verbally by Saint-Preux during his tutorship of Julie. We have seen that in her long letter number eighteen of part three, Julie had prodded Saint-Preux to pray: "Adore the Supreme Being, my worthy and prudent friend."[31] But Saint-Preux was unable to resort to prayer in his state of depression ("accablement"). His pain led him rather to consider suicide as a solution to his misfortune, later replaced by a long trip. Now, Julie, secure in her own family, tried to talk Saint-Preux into marrying her cousin, Claire d'Orbe, who had become widowed, and thereby find happiness himself too. Julie is using all the arguments against celibacy that she feels are convincing and the letter could have ended on that note. However, as she persists and asks him to think the matter over carefully, she suddenly and unabashedly suggests that he resort to the greatest fount of wisdom: religion and, more specifically, prayer. It is at this point that there begins a discussion on the

---

[30] Cf. Letter VII, Part 6, *O.C.* II, 674.

[31] Ibid., p. 358.

nature and efficacy of prayer. Some critics, like Mornet[32] qualify this discussion as a digression, since the theme of the novel does not call for it. True enough. But Julie feels that religion and prayer may help him as they have helped her and, no doubt, she wishes the possible marriage of Saint-Preux and her cousin to be as successful as hers by having "recourse to prayer in solitude."[33] In addition, Mornet himself suggests that the purpose of the second part of the book was an after-thought of Rousseau and more specifically the sixth section was written precisely to oppose[34] to the philosophical and materialistic rationalism of the period the religion of Julie and proposing that it is true because it is "amiable and moving."[35] Moreover, discussions on prayers of request and of adoration were frequent in Rousseau's time and so it was natural for him to include them in his novel. Be that as it may, he here has Julie open the discussion. She refers to Saint-Preux's previous views on the topic, views which, as we have said, we know only from Julie's sixth letter of the sixth part of this novel and not directly from Saint-Preux. Now, she tries to refute his views.

What irks Julie first is that his refusal to resort to petitionary prayer is due to his excessive sense of pride, his "philosophical haughtiness "[36] that disdains the "simplicity of the Christian"[37] which she finds important to preserve because "she sees in it an act of humility, a way of maintaining in our soul the sentiment of our weakness."[38] Later, she will write: "Let us be humble.[39]

Julie says that Saint-Preux had also mentioned to her that prayers of petition were useless, for God gave us in our conscience the notions of what is right and the freedom to choose it. Julie retorts that, free as we are, we are weak and need Divine assistance to choose right. And

---

[32] Cf. Mornet, p. 263.

[33] Charles W. Hendel, *J.-J. Rousseau Moralist* (Indianapolis, New York: The Library of Liberal Arts, published by Bobbs-Merrill, 1934), II, 53.

[34] Cf. Mornet, pp. 263–64.

[35] Ibid., p. 264.

[36] Cf. *O.C.* II, 672.

[37] Ibid.

[38] Cf. Gouhier, p. 123.

[39] Cf. *O.C.* II, 672.

how can we obtain it if we do not deign to ask for it?[40] Prayer is then "a necessary supplement to the self-reliant conscience of man."[41]

The next argument of Saint-Preux is that it might be an embarrassment to God to watch over each individual and relate to him in prayer and probably a presumptuousness on our part to expect that of God—in other words "scorning a too human conception of the Deity"[47] from which he deduces that God operates by general laws. Julie's reply is that it is rather he, Saint-Preux, who is applying human criteria to Divinity, that since man's capacity for love of others is limited, he proceeds by "induction" from human experience[43] that so is God's which, of course, is non-commensurate, as God is the ideal of perfection and can do what man cannot do. Rousseau's belief in a personal Providence in which he departs from deism is at the core of Julie's argument here. Observes Burgelin: Rousseau "loathes the idea of an impersonal force that would govern the world."[44] It is here, too, that Julie adds her quip:. "O great *philosophes*! how obliged God must be to you for having provided him with convenient methods and for having reduced His labor."[45] Let us also keep in mind that the discovery of Newton on the vastness of the universe may well be in the background of Saint Preux's objection.

---

[40] Cf. Letter VI, Part 6, *O.C.* II, 672: "Nous sommes libres, il est vrai, mais nous sommes ignorants, faibles, portés au mal et d'où nous viendraient la lumière et la force, si ce n'est de celui qui en est la source, et pourquoi les obtiendrons-nous si nous ne daignons pas les demander?"

[41] Cf. Hendel, p. 53.

[42] Ibid.

[43] Ibid.

[44] Pierre Burgelin, *La Philosophie de l'existence de J.-J. Rousseau* (Paris: Presses universitaires de France, 1952), p. 457.

[45] Cf. *O.C.* 11, 672: "O grands philosophes! que Dieu vous est obligé de lui fournir ainsi des méthodes commodes, et de lui abréger le travail."

Finally, Saint-Preux holds the view that God knows our needs[46] and He knows best. Our prayers of petition are, therefore, at least superfluous. To which Julie answers that the greatest need we have is precisely to know our needs.[47] We become then aware of our dependence on Providence to let us know our needs, so that we may act on them and avoid misery: "Our greatest need, the only one which we are able to attend to, is to be aware of our needs; and the first step for getting out of our misery is to know it. Let us be humble in order to be wise; let us face our weakness and we will be strong."[48] As Burgelin conceptualizes it: "We can expect prayer to give us the awareness and the strength of what we are."[49]

Of course, equally part of Julie's conception of prayer, is what she said in letter eighteen of the third section right after her marriage: "The same helping hand which has led me across the darkness has also removed from my eyes the veil of error. and has returned me to myself, despite myself."[50] Conceptualizing this statement, Burgelin

---

[46] Cf. Isaiah lcv. 24: "And it shall come to pass that, before they call, I will answer" and the comment on it in the *Midrash* (explanation of Biblical text from the ethical and devotional points of view): "A human being can judge correctly only if he hears the case presented to him. God, however, is not so. He knows what is in a person's heart before that person puts it into words," *Midrash Rabbah on Exodus* (Tel Aviv: A. Halevy, 1959), III, 276–77. Obviously, Isaiah and the *Midrash* draw different conclusions from it than Saint-Preux.

[47] A parallel idea to Julie's is found in Bachya Ibn Pakudah, eleventh-century Spanish-Jewish ethical philosopher, in his work *Duties of the Heart*, quoted by Joseph H. Hertz in *A Book of Jewish Thoughts* (New York: Bloch, 1953), p. 172: "O God, I stand before Thee knowing all my deficiencies and overwhelmed by Thy greatness and majesty…. Thou knowest best what is for my good. If I recite my wants, it is not to remind Thee of them, but only so that I may understand better how great is my dependence upon Thee."

[48] Cf.Letter VI, Part 6, *O.C.* II, 672–73: "Le plus grand de nos besoins, le seul auquel nous pouvons pourvoir, est celui de sentir nos besoins; et le premier pas pour sortir de notre misère est de la connaître. Soyons humbles pour être sages; voyons notre faiblesse, et nous serons forts."

[49] Cf. Burgelin, *La Philosophie de l'existence de J.-J. Rousseau*, p. 462: "Nous pouvons attendre de la prière la conscience de ce que nous sommes et la force."

[50] Cf. Letter XVIII, Part 3, *O.C.* II, 356: "La main secourable qui m'a conduite à travers les ténèbres est celle qui lève à mes yeux le voile de l'erreur et me rend à moi, malgré moi-même."

writes: "The function of prayer is to help us find again our true personality under the gaze of God."[51]

And Julie concludes letter six of the sixth section with an exhortation to Saint-Preux to take counsel in difficult times not only from himself but rather from a higher power. For man, in her judgment, is too subjective and limited while God is objective and sees better what is good for us, not only for the moment but for the future as well.

E. Saint-Preux's Defense of his Position on Prayer and his Conception of Prayer

In letter seven of the sixth section of *La Nouvelle Héloïse*, Saint-Preux replies to the preceding letter by Julie and he does so in a manner similar to her letter. He first speaks at some length of the renewal of their correspondence and of her proposal that he marry her cousin Claire—which he declines to do—and then devotes the rest of the letter to discussing prayer and answering her criticism of his position.

Julie had reproached him with the use of analogy from human weakness which he applied to God to prove that God proceeds by general and not particular providence and, therefore, his conclusion that God is not relating to individuals in prayer. Saint-Preux foreshadows modern thought in claiming that we have to resort to analogy, for how else except by the method of induction can one judge what we do not know from what we do know. It also so happens, he assures us, that all analogies show the operation of general laws and, so does reason. Yet, by analogy, we may get the wrong answers, too, even about the knowable and God is by nature beyond the knowable. So Julie is right in refuting the use of analogy. As for Julie's arguments, he disposes of them in the following manner:

> For, while it is true that His power has no need of a method for shortening His work, it is worthy of His wisdom, however, to prefer the ways that are most simple, to the end that there is nothing unnecessary in the means any

---

[51] Cf. Burgelin, *La Philosophie de l'existence de J.-J. Rousseau*, p. 462: "Le rôle de la prière est de nous aider à retrouver, sous le regard de Dieu, notre vraie personne."

more than in the results. In creating man, He has endowed him with all the faculties necessary for the accomplishing of what He requires of him; and when we beseech Him to give us the power to do good, we ask for nothing but what He has already given us. He has given us reason, so that we may know what is good, conscience so that we may love it,[52] and liberty in order that we may choose it. It is in these sublime gifts that Divine grace consists, and as we have received them all we are held accountable for the use of them all.[53]

Petitionary prayers ask God for favors. Saint-Preux has taken exception to such prayers.[54] Here, he reiterates his belief that God does

---

[52] In a footnote to his edition of *Julie ou La Nouvelle Héloïse* (p. 671), Pomeau perspicaciously notes that "Saint-Preux makes of the moral conscience a sentiment and not a judgment, which is against the definitions of the *philosophes*. I believe that in this, their so-called fellow in thought ("confrère") is–right."

[53] LetterVII, Part 6, *O.C.* II, 683: "Car bien que sa puissance n'ait pas besoin de méthode pour abréger le travail, il est digne de sa sagesse de préférer pourtant les voies les plus simples, afin qu'il n'y ait rien d'inutile dans les moyens non plus que dans les effets. En créant l'homme, il l'a doué de toutes les facultés nécessaires pour accomplir ce qu'il exigeait de lui, et quand nous lui demandons le pouvoir de bien faire, nous ne lui demandons rien qu'il ne nous ait déjà donné. Il nous a donné la raison pour connaître ce qui est bien, la conscience pour l'aimer, et la liberté pour le choisir. C'est dans ces dons sublimes que consiste la grâce divine, et comme nous les avons tous reçus, nous en sommes tous comptables." See also Hendel, II, 54. Saint-Preux has said in the above lines that Divine grace consists in three gifts: reason, conscience and liberty. F.C. Green in his *J.-J. Rousseau—A Critical Study of His Life and Writings*, p. 199, gives us the origin and the implications of this view on grace: "Here, Saint-Preux merely summarizes the views of Fénelon who says that life is a continual grace. Saint-Preux implies that Julie had no need of an 'inner revolution,' of an infusion of supernatural grace; she had only to follow the deepest instincts of her own nature in order to be impeccable. That is of course sheer Pelagianism."

[54] It may be of some interest to see how this problem of petitionary prayers is treated in another faith-community. In the daily Hebrew worship, the central portion which is identified with prayer ("Tefilah") itself is called the *Amidah*, meaning "standing," because it is recited in a reverent, standing position, with feet joined, at attention. Its nineteen weekday blessings comprise three of praise at the beginning, three of thanksgiving at the end, and the thirteen middle ones dealing with communal, public needs, such as knowledge, health, economic well-being, forgiveness, righteous administration of justice etc. All are couched in the plural and individual needs are expressed as part of the larger, social needs. On the Sabbath, however, the thirteen middle, petitionary blessings are replaced by one single blessing which deals only with praise of God for the gift of the Sabbath-day because no needs are to be mentioned on the weekly

not do special or extraordinary favors to anyone for He has well provided for the needs of man. Moreover, such acts would be contrary to Divine justice, and between Divine omnipotence and Divine justice, we know that Jean-Jacques clearly opts for justice. Does it follow then that prayer is useless? Saint-Preux asks himself. And he replies in the negative. Prayer is not useless, but the spiritual change is produced solely by us and within us, as we raise ourselves to God in prayer— on that he is most emphatic. In the words of Saint-Preux: "By imploring His help, we learn to find it ourselves. It is not He who changes us, it is we who change by raising ourselves to Him. Everything that one requests properly, one gives to oneself and, as you have said it, one increases one's strength by recognizing one's weakness."[55] Saint-Preux then does not reject prayer, even prayer of petition,[56] but regards any benefit achieved by prayer as originating with the praying individual himself.

Let us pause here for a few moments and examine what Saint-Preux means by his assertion that "we change by raising ourselves to Him." This certainly applies to prayers of adoration and praise. Saint-Preux also seems to extend this concept of prayer to that smaller part of petitionary prayers in which the very act of praying can by itself help, as in requests for improvement, elevation, strength against weaknesses and temptation, determination to do right—all these being requests for moral, spiritual and inspirational strength in exercising well our freedom of will and action. However, there remains the vast area of concrete needs (health, livelihood, children, long life, res-

---

hallowed day. The same is true about holidays. Moreover, following a Talmudic ruling that "a man should always first recount the praise of God and then pray" (*Berakhoth*, 32a), the initial portion of the Jewish daily morning service is composed of *Pesuké d'Zimrah* ("verses of song, of praise") expressing God's majesty, love and power as displayed in nature and in Biblical history.

[55] Cf. Letter VII, Part 6, *O.C.* II, 684–85: "En implorant son secours, nous apprenons à le trouver. Ce n'est pas lui qui nous change, c'est nous qui changeons en nous élevant à lui. Tout ce qu'on lui demande comme il faut, on se le donne, et, comme vous l'avez dit, on augmente sa force en reconnaissant sa faiblesse."

[56] Cf. Mornet, p. 269. However, F.C. Green in his *J.-J. Rousseau—A Critical Study of His Life and Writings*, p. 254, says that "whilst condemning prayers of petition, he [Saint-Preux] concedes that prayer itself is useful." We do not see this distinction and feel that Saint-Preux does accept prayer of petition in a limited sense as we shall now discuss.

cue from danger etc.) where the act of prayer in itself cannot help and Divine intervention is sought. This type of petitionary prayer is not discussed by Saint-Preux. Is it avoided intentionally? We cannot tell. We do know, however, that in crisis situations, direct intervention by a personal Providence will be solicited by both Julie and Jean-Jacques. We may explain these as resulting from Rousseau's return, when troubled, to earlier modes of expression when he used traditional prayer. However, he avoids any Christological references even then, so perhaps, they, too, reflect Rousseau's theism which accepts a personal Providence to which one may turn even with real, concrete petitionary prayers. With this in mind, we can see how Julie and Saint-Preux both agree on the efficacy of prayer, since they discuss the "abstract" category of prayers (requests for moral, spiritual and inspirational strength) and only disagree on the means whereby the object of the prayer is achieved: whether Providence grants it in response to our prayer (Julie)or we give it to ourselves (Saint-Preux).

A possible view of Saint-Preux's stand on prayers of petition to God for concrete needs may be that Saint-Preux did not really avoid discussing them. Rather, he applies to them, too, his belief that it is "we who change by raising ourselves to Him," and since we change, we emerge as renewed personalities with a better perspective and a better perception of our needs which, psychosomatically, has a beneficent effect on our being. Julie, however, might argue, we suggest, that since we change, there is a corresponding change in the attitude of Divinity to the renewed person that we have become. This is sheer justice on the part of a just God to give to the new and better man what he now deserves. God has not changed His mind. He has rightly adjusted His response to the new condition of the praying man.

The problem of man's repentance and Divine forgiveness has also been left out, though we may surmise the respective positions of Julie and Saint-Preux to be similar to those taken with reference to the "abstract" category of prayers which we just mentioned. In general, though, the petitionary prayer asks God to have His mercy overrule His justice toward us, and forgive our action which may have called for just punishment or for withholding of benefits we desire. In that sense, we do not ask God to change His mind, as it were, but to temper His justice with His mercy.[57] No change of mind is required of God in order to forgive.

Deserving of mention at this point is Burgelin's observation of a belief of Saint-Preux shared also by Julie, namely that prayer helps us to discover, under the gaze of God, our true personality:[58] "All the acts of understanding which raise us toward God carry us above ourselves . . . it is we who change by raising ourselves to Him. "[59]

Let us return to Saint-Preux's discussion of Julie's letter. While seeing value in prayer, Saint-Preux nonetheless sharply warns Julie that the abuse of prayer can easily lead to mystic ecstasies which he finds dangerous: "But if we abuse prayer and become mystics, we lose our way as a result of our effort to rise ever higher; by looking for Divine grace, we renounce reason; to obtain a gift from heaven, we trample under foot another gift; by persisting in our wish that God illumine us, we deprive ourselves of the lights which He has given us. Who are we to want to force God to perform a miracle?"[60] The burden

---

[57] One example from the Bible will suffice to point out this concept of forgiveness at the request of man: "And the Lord said: 'I pardon as thou hast asked'" (Numbers, xiv.20). Man's entreaty to have God judge us with mercy rather than strict justice is supplemented by God's desire to treat us with compassion. Thus, the Talmud ascribes to God Himself the following prayer: "May it be My will that My mercy may overcome My anger, and that My mercy may prevail over My [other] attributes, so that I may deal with My children in the attribute of mercy and, on their behalf, stop short of the limit of strict justice" (tractate of *Berakhoth*, p. 7a).

[58] Cf. Burgelin, *La Philosophie de l'existence de J.-J. Rousseau*, p. 462.

[59] Cf. Letter VII, Part 6, O.C. II, 684: "Tous les actes de l'entendement qui nous élèvent à Dieu nous portent au-dessus de nous-mêmes…c'est nous qui changeons en nous élevant à lui."

[60] Ibid., p. 685: "Mais si l'on abuse de l'oraison et qu'on devienne mystique, on se perd à force de s'élever; en cherchant la grâce, on renonce à la raison; pour obtenir un don du ciel, on en foule aux pieds un autre; en s'obstinant à vouloir qu'il nous éclaire, on s'ôte les lumières qu'il nous a données. Qui sommes-nous pour vouloir forcer Dieu de faire un miracle?" This last sentence stating that it is an act of human presumption to want to force God's hand to perform a miracle for us is also a concept expressed in the Talmud (tractate of *Shabbat*, p. 53b) by the sage Abaya: "How lowly was this man that the order of nature was changed on his account." The classical Hebrew mind considers the natural order marvelous and "miraculous" enough without having to resort to supernatural phenomena. In-

of this warning by Saint-Preux is that we should operate on a rational level first and foremost. There is also in this warning an element of fear of man overreaching himself and, as a result, losing contact with reality and rationality in order to venture on the unchartered seas of mysticism. F.C. Green explains to us what mysticism meant in Rousseau's context: "By 'mystic state' ('état mystique'), Rousseau obviously means the state of quietude or 'mystic prayer' ('oraison mystique') familiar to Mme Guyon and other disciples of Molinos. These Quietists claimed that once the soul was closely united with God, it should remain in a state of perfect quietude, surrendering utterly to the movement of the Divine spirit; and 'whilst the higher part of the soul is in this holy repose, it must not trouble itself about what is happening to its imagination or even to its body.' This is the kind of *oraison* which Saint-Preux has in mind when he warns Julie that by abusing the habit of prayer, we drift into mysticism because, in seeking to uplift ourselves to God, we relinquish the intellectual powers given us by Him."[61]

In this seventh letter (of part six of the book), when Saint-Preux began talking about prayer, he had cautioned Julie that her devotion might lead her to menacing quietism. Now that he has amended his concept of prayer and sees some usefulness in it, he probably senses that his approval of prayer might become an additional inducement to Julie, who is well inclined to it, to indulge more frequently and more freely in prayer. He, therefore, returns to this theme of mysticism and feels impelled to warn her in very strong terms not to overindulge in it.

He starts by positing a general truism: "There is nothing so good that when done in excess does not become blameworthy," and immediately applies it to "even devotion which, in excess, turns into delirium."[62] He reassures her that her devotion is too pure to reach that extreme. Yet, he fears she might be on the way to it. He therefore cautions her to watch the beginning of the excess of devotion while it can

---

deed, it makes a good man "lowly" to have God change the natural order for him.

[61]   Cf. F.C. Green, pp. 254–55.

[62]   Cf. *O.C.* 11, 685: "Il n'y a rien de bien qui n'ait un excès blâmable; même la dévotion qui tourne en délire."

still be controlled. He also reminds her of her having blamed in the past the ecstasies of ascetics. Those ecstasies, he cautions us, are produced by gradually extending the time allotted to prayer beyond what human endurance ("faiblesse") permits. Then, the excess of time spent in prayer "exhausts the spirit, lights up the imagination, and creates visions, so that one becomes inspired, prophetic and is on the way to fanaticism."[63] Burgelin notes: "The worst evil is, therefore, fanaticism, the spirit of exclusion."[64] Naturally, fanaticism is an evil. We feel, however, that Burgelin should have pursued Saint-Preux further in this letter, for then he would have perceived the ominous specter of Muralt whose mental health was in the end affected by a visionary, Mme Dorothée. Saint-Preux describes the symptoms of devotion in Julie and appeals to her not to become a *dévote*, term used here in a pejorative sense: "You lock yourself up frequently in your room, you meditate, you pray ceaselessly: you have not yet joined the company of the pietists but you read their books, I have never blamed your taste for the writings of the good Fénelon: but what have you got to do with those of his disciple [Mme Guyon]? You read Muralt, I read him too; but choose his *Lettres* and you choose his *Instinct divin*. See what has become of him, deplore the aberration of this wise man and think about yourself. Pious and Christian woman, are you going to be nothing more than a *dévote*?"[65] Moderation in prayer is then advocated by Saint-Preux as good wisdom, good religion and good mental health as well.

To sum up, it seems to us that the deism of Saint-Preux leading him to stress transcendence as opposed to immanence continues to lead him to maintain distance between God and man, in order to

---

[63] Ibid., p. 685: "L'esprit s'épuise, l'imagination s'allume et donne des visions, on devient inspiré, prophète, et il n'y a plus ni sens ni génie qui garantisse du fanatisme."

[64] Cf. Surgelin, *La Philosophie de l'existence de J.-J. Rousseau*, p. 466.

[65] Cf.O.C. II, 685: "Vous vous enfermez fréquemment dans votre cabinet, vous vous recueillez, vous priez sans cesse; vous ne voyez pas encore les piétistes, mais vous lisez leurs livres. Je n'ai jamais blâmé votre goût pour les écrits du bon Fénelon: mais que faites-vous de ceux de sa disciple [Mme Guyon]?Vous lisez Muralt, je le lis aussi; mais je choisis ses Lettres, et vous choisissez son *Instinct divin*. Voyez comment il a fini, déplorez les égarements de cet homme sage, et songez à vous. Femme pieuse et chrétienne, allez-vous n'être plus qu'une dévote?"

avoid an excess of ecstasy and mystical absorption into Deity which he fears as unhealthy and also unwarranted by religion. Saint-Preux clearly belongs to the eighteenth century, though he accepts religion and prayer in a period that questions both. He does so, however, with reservations, avoiding what he considers as excesses.

F. New Answer of Julie about Prayer and its Advantages—and a Paean

How will Julie react to the criticism of Saint-Preux? In the very next letter (sixth part, letter eight), we have her reply. She begins with his accusation about her "so-called devotion"[66] and she asks: "If devotion is good, why should I be blamed for it?"[67] She sees no reason for blame from her viewpoint. Only to philosophers is devotion "too low" a term, something which she bemoans: "Philosophical dignity disdains a vulgar cult; it wants to serve God more nobly; it raises its pretensions and its pride to heaven itself. O, my poor philosophers!"[68] And a little further, she states: "Before you deprive me of the guide I have chosen, give me another upon which I could depend."[69] Wherefrom, she goes into a lengthy review of what happened to her in order to prove the value of prayer, even prayer of devotion. She had relied on her own lights and feelings and she had failed despite her love for virtue and her having been *bien née*. Yet, others have lived more prudently than she. What do they have that she lacked? The answer is that they have better inner resources, or as she puts it: "They must have had a better support."[70] The others have one more advantage: besides desire, they have hope too. When desire erupts, they do not require immediate fulfillment. Hope helps them to bear for a longer time the torment of passion. Furthermore, hope, imagination and illusion can provide greater happiness than the reality of the fulfillment itself. For expectation, or what she calls the

---

[66] Cf. Letter VIII, Part 6, *O.C.* II, 689: "prétendue dévotion."
[67] Ibid., p. 692: "Si la dévotion est bonne, où est le tort d'en avoir?"
[68] Ibid., p. 692.
[69] Ibid.
[70] Ibid., 693: "Elles ont un meilleur appui."

"pleasure of desiring" ("plaisir de désirer"), exceeds gratification. That feeling of expectation and of postponement of wish for immediate gratification is developed by those who have the moral strength to stand and wait and is the result of religion and prayer.

Having discovered in her past experience the value of expectation and of inner moral strength which are fostered by prayer, Julie now turns her attention to her present state of contentment and fulfillment. Suddenly, amidst all her bliss, she senses within herself something lacking. She writes: "There remains in my heart an unutilized force for which it sees no outlet....My friend, I am, indeed, too happy; happiness bores me."[71] And further: "I am constantly uneasy; my heart knows not what it lacks; it knows not what it desires."[72] Julie identifies this new and strange emotion she experiences as "disgust with well-being"[73] which F.C. Green calls "the ennui that comes from a happiness so complete as to leave nothing more in life to be desired."[74] Julie describes it for Saint-Preux in the following manner:

> Finding, therefore, nothing to satisfy it here below, my starving soul seeks its nourishment elsewhere. By uplifting itself to the source of all feeling and being, it loses there its aridity and languor: there it is reborn, reanimated; there it finds a new recharge; from there it draws new life; there it acquires another existence which does not depend on the passions of the body; or rather, it is no longer inside myself; instead, it becomes wholly immersed in the Infinite Being whom it contemplates and, momentarily freed of its bonds, consoles itself for having to reassume them by this preliminary experience of a more sublime state which, it hopes, will one day be its own.[75]

---

71 Ibid., p. 694: "Il lui [au coeur] reste une force inutile dont il ne sait que faire....Mon ami, je suis trop heureuse; le bonheur m'ennuie."

72 Ibid., p. 694: "j'y vis inquiète; mon coeur ignore ce qu'il lui manque; il désire sans savoir quoi!"

73 Cf. Van Tieghem, p. 58: "Avant Chateaubriand, on ne trouve nulle part mieux exprimé ce 'dégoût du bien-être' qui s'empare de Julie."

74 Cf. F.C. Green, p. 200.

75 Cf. O.C. II, 694–95: "Ne trouvant donc rien ici-bas qui lui suffise, mon âme avide cherche ailleurs de quoi la remplir; en s'élevant à la source du sentiment et de l'être, elle y perd sa sécheresse et sa langueur: elle y renaît, elle s'y ranime, elle y trouve un nouveau ressort, elle y puise une nouvelle vie; elle y prend une autre existence qui ne tient point aux passions du corps, ou plutôt elle n'est plus en moi-même; elle est toute dans l'Etre immense qu'elle contemple, et dégagée un

While this description does not reflect yet a profound mystical experience, Saint-Preux's caution to her is justified, for she is on the way to such an experience if the practice be continued regularly and for gradually longer periods of time. Analyzing the novel up to this point indicates a rise in the frequency and quality of prayer of Julie with a possibility of her doing so in the tradition of the mystics.

While we cannot really know what Rousseau had in mind in ascribing to Julie a gnawing boredom ("ennui") and emptiness which she seeks to overcome by prayer, it may be very enlightening to bring here the insights of Dr. Joseph B. Soloveitchik into boredom amidst plenty in our time presented in an unpublished lecture at Yeshiva University). He starts out with Kierkegaard's thesis that boredom is the basic disease of modern man. It comes as a result of the feeling of emptiness, purposelessness and absurdity of existence itself. It is a metaphysical experience. It is felt more poignantly by people of greater intelligence and sensitivity. It is rooted in man's essence. It is existential and not social or economic in origin. While the surface external crisis can be actively combatted and overcome, there is no solution to the depth crisis except through prayer. Rousseau may well have had intimations of this nature when he portrayed Julie as subject to this kind of predicament amidst material and social plenty and had her turn to deep, almost mystical prayer for relief.

The last letter of dying Julie to Saint-Preux (sixth part, letter XII), forwarded to him by M. de Wolmar, abruptly changes our perspective. For there we learn in an open confession of Julie that she still loves him and not like a brother and, what is significant, she admits that she had lived under an illusion and that "one day more, perhaps, and I might have been guilty" and, therefore, "I leave at the right time."[76] In the light of this last letter of Julie, her experience described in letter eight under discussion is correctly called "pseudo-mystic élan" by F. C. Green, "pseudo" for "hers is not a truly mystic soul which has eliminated from its substance all that is earthly and impure

---

moment de ses entraves, elle se console d'y rentrer par cet essai d'un état plus sublime qu'elle espère être un jour le sien."

[76] Ibid., p. 741: "Un jour de plus, peut-être, et j'étais coupable!...je pars au moment favorable."

so as to become God's instrument. "[77] Mornet, too, views it so when he writes: "When Julie is about to die, she understands that it is time that she die; she confesses it to herself, she confesses her incurable love. She confesses at the same time that her attempt of loving friendship was absurd, that the second part of the novel is but a paradox."[78] This sudden upsetting effect of a few lines in Julie's last letter to Saint-Preux, it seems to us, could have been left out and the novel would have been more unified in its theme. In adding those lines, Jean-Jacques may merely be reflecting his personal dream and hope that he can make up with Sophie d'Houdetot and her lover, Saint-Lambert, in a kind of unusual *ménage à trois* and he transposes this in his novel, with him being not a lover but a moral guide, a brother. They do not seem to blend well with the body of the book.

Coming back to letter eight, Julie admits that her present views on mystical ecstasy conflict with her past disapproval of it. In her defense, she says only that she had never experienced it before while now she does. Without feeling any need to justify herself, she merely adds: "I only say that it is sweet, that it makes up for the feeling that my happiness is dwindling away, that it fills the emptiness of the soul and that it casts a new interest on life spent to deserve it."[79] If it produces something evil, it no doubt should be rejected, says Julie, but these words are not written very convincingly for Julie is already attached to mystical ecstasy. Moreover, it is superior to philosophy for it promotes virtue and happiness, ideas which, incidentally, will antagonize still more the *philosophes*. Basically, she adopts the pragmatic solution when she writes to Saint-Preux: "Either leave me in this state which I find agreeable or show me how I can fare better."[80]

Concerning the ecstasies of the mystics, Julie says she disapproved of them before and she does so now, but her disapproval is not a complete one for she immediately qualifies it—when they de-

---

77   Cf. F.C. Green, p. 200.

78   Cf. Mornet, p. 35.

79   Cf. O.C. II, 695: "je dis seulement qu'il est doux, qu'il supplée au sentiment du bonheur qui s'épuise, qu'il remplit le vide de l'âme, et qu'il jette un nouvel intérêt sur la vie passée à le mériter."

80   Ibid., p. 695: "Ou laissez-moi dans un état qui m'est agréable, ou montrez-moi comment je puis être mieux."

tach us from our duties and, by the charms of contemplation, lead us to quietism. As for herself, despite Saint-Preux's misgivings, she feels she is far from it. Wishing to reinforce that point, she stresses the centrality of the active life and of duties duly performed: "I know full well that to serve God does not mean to spend our lives' on our knees, praying; it means, rather, to fulfill on earth the duties which He imposes on us.[81] She also quotes Metastasio on the paramount role of duty[82] and states her own position: "First of all, we ought to perform our duties and then pray when we can. This is the rule I try to follow."[83] Having refuted Saint-Preux's contention about devotion by agreeing with his fear of abuses, she has come to the point of asserting that in her case duty comes first and prayer second and that with a qualification "when one can." This seems to us to be simply a tactical response in order to safeguard the acceptability of some part of devotion to Saint-Preux.

A few paragraphs above, Julie had said that her soul had a need to be "wholly immersed in the Infinite Being whom it contemplates" which expresses a striving for mystical union of the human soul with Divinity. She subsequently devaluates her practice of prayer to take second place after fulfillment of one's duties and then only limiting it to a pragmatic "when one can," sporadically. Then, she further reduces prayer to a "recreation," and finally still further reducing it to one of her many "pleasures" that are at her disposal, with the additional qualification that among her pleasures, prayer is "the most sensible and the most innocent of all. "[84] As Julie continues writing her letter, it appears ever more clearly that what she has just said about prayer, deescalating it from a means of the soul's absorption into Divinity (mysticism) to being one of many pleasures (mundane term)

---

[81]   Ibid., p. 695: "Servir Dieu, ce n'est point passer sa vie à genoux dans un oratoire, je le sais bien; c'est remplir sur la terre les devoirs qu'il nous impose."

[82]   Ibid., p. 695, citation of Metastasio (Métastase in French), *La Morte d'Abele*, first part with French translation made by Rousseau and reading: "Le coeur lui suffit et qui fait son devoir le prie" (*O.C.*, p. 1788, note d). Quoted by Pomeau, *Julie ou La Nouvelle Héloïse*, p. 684, note. Rhymed English translation: "To have a heart that glows with pure desire, / To love and serve where duty may require."

[83]   Ibid., p. 695: 'Il faut premièrement faire ce qu'on doit, et puis prier quand on le peut. Voilà la règle que je tâche de suivre."

[84]   Ibid., p. 696: "le plus sensible et le plus innocent de tous."

was in self-defense vis-à-vis Saint-Preux. For she has taken seriously the warning of her former tutor, as is apparent from the statement that follows and in which she says that she has examined herself with great care since receiving his letter and that she has studied the effects on her of an inclination that seems so strongly to displease him, but that she has found nothing, so far, to make her worry about a possible abuse of her supposed poorly understood devotion. In the same self-defensive, apologetic tone, she tries to diminish the importance of prayer to her by insisting that she does not have for that exercise too lively a taste which would make her suffer when deprived of it. In other words, she has reached in her apology the point "zero" in prayer, with deprivation not affecting her. What a quick descent from the need for a mystical union with the Infinite Being! Her use of an ordinal number ("first") shows her intent to make a rational, orderly refutation of his accusation or rather insinuation as to her being a devotee. But it is not followed by the succeeding ordinal numbers, though the ideas in her letter progress. The reason seems to be that an influx of emotion invades her writing as she admits that, in stress-situations, she resorts to her private room "sometimes" to find calm and peace in prayer. Here, too, she hastens to add apologetically lest that be misunderstood by Saint-Preux: "I require neither frequent nor long intervals of solitude,"[85] and, in cases of persistent sadness, a few tears bring her "instant" relief. That deescalation, we feel, represents her apologia and not her present belief.

Let us take note here that Julie's place for prayer is not the Protestant Temple but rather her private home, her "cabinet." Let us also note the direct communication between her and Divinity and the absence of even the slightest mention so far of a minister or any intermediary or spiritual guide. These are part of the deist tradition. Julie also tells us to whom she addresses her prayers: "The God I serve is a merciful God, a Father: what moves me most is His goodness; that surpasses in my eyes all His other attributes; it is the only one I really perceive."[86] It is so, perhaps, because goodness is the only attribute

---

[85] Ibid., p. 696: "Il ne me faut des séances ni fréquentes ni longues."

[86] Ibid., p. 696: "Le Dieu que je sers est un Dieu clément, un père: ce qui me touche est sa bonté; elle efface à mes yeux tous ses autres attributs; elle est le seul que je conçois."

she herself could appeal to with a chance of obtaining mercy, forgiveness and peace of mind. However, she is well aware of the other attributes as the next sentence reveals. The dots after "justice" are particularly meaningful, for she fears that attribute which demands of man to comply with high standards of behavior and, therefore, does not want to elaborate on it and on punishment to which it may lead. In its stead, she turns it around and makes God's justice a reason for Divine compassion toward human weakness. In the words of Julie: "His power astonishes me; His infinity confounds me, His justice…Well, He has made man weak; so since He is just, He must be merciful. "[87] Her greatest source of consolation—so important to Rousseau as well—lies in the thought that God knows our human limitations. After having come to terms with the Divine attribute of justice which she feared, Julie confronts the concept of Divine retribution. She says: "The vengeful God is the God of the wicked; I can neither fear Him for myself nor beseech Him against someone else."[88] Unable to reconcile or re-interpret this concept to suit her views, she simply dismisses it. Julie can accept God only on her own terms. Then, she bursts out with a paean in which her piety comes to the fore: "O God of peace, God of goodness, it is Thee that I adore! I feel that I am the work of Thy hands; and I hope that at the last judgment I will find Thee such as Thou hast manifested Thyself to my heart in my lifetime."[89]

Finding reassurance in the prayer that it is the God of goodness who will judge her in the next world, Julie enumerates some of the practical effects of prayer: it adds sweetness to her days and joy to her heart, she feels lighter and gayer, and life is made smoother, less rough, less "angular"; she is in a better mood that even her husband appreciates and he comes to regard her devotion as opium for the soul—good if indulged in moderation.

---

[87] Ibid., p. 696: "Sa puissance m'étonne, son immensité me confond, sa justice…il a fait l'homme faible; puisqu'il est juste; il est clément."

[88] Ibid., p. 696: "Le Dieu vengeur est le Dieu des méchants; je ne puis ni le craindre pour moi, ni l'implorer contre un autre."

[89] Ibid., p. 696: "O Dieu de paix, Dieu de bonté, c'est toi que j'adore! c'est de toi, je le sens, que je suis l'ouvrage; et j'espère te retrouver au dernier jugement tel que tu parles à mon coeur durant ma vie."

Then, Julie voices her aversion for the abuses of devotion. Madame Guyon would have done better if she had concentrated on fulfilling her duties as a mother instead of composing books on devotion, argue about them with bishops and be put into the Bastille for dreams which no one understands anyway. Julie then discourses against the mystical, and figurative language which feeds the heart with chimeras of the imagination and presents a danger to those who have a tender heart and a lively imagination.[90] However, what shocks Julie most is the lack of humanity of those whom she calls "professional *dévots*" ("dévots de profession"). The passage is worth quoting in its entirety:

> But what has alienated me most from these dévots by profession is that acerbity of manner which renders them insensitive to humanity; it is that excessive pride which makes them look down with pity upon the rest of mankind. If ever they condescend to stoop from their imaginary elevation to do an act of kindness, it is done in such a humiliating way, their pity is expressed in such a cruel tone, their justice is so rigid, their charity is so harsh, their zeal so bitter, their contempt resembles hatred so very much, that even the insensitivity of other people is less cruel than their pity. Their love of God serves them as an excuse for loving nobody; they do not even love each other. Does one ever see true friendship among the *dévots*? But the more they detach themselves from people, the more they demand from them; and one might say that they only elevate themselves to God in order to exercise His authority over the rest of His creatures.[91]

---

[90] A footnote by Rousseau in *O.C.* II, 697, has Julie say that, if it were possible, she would excise the "Song of Songs" from the Biblical canon, something which, incidentally, Jewish sages wanted to do, but the Men of the Great Assembly (500–300 before the common era) admitted it into the Hagiographa (*Avoth d'Rabbi Nathan*, first of the minor tractates of the Talmud, ch. I, p. 4a). Later, when the issue was discussed again, Rabbi Akiba asserted: "All the ages are not worth the day on which the "Song of Songs" was given to Israel; for all the Writings [i.e. Hagiographa] are holy, but the "Song of Songs" is the Holy of the Holies" (Mishnah-*Yaddayim* III, 5). Interestingly, Rabbi Akiba, the great intellect, was also the great mystic who came out unhurt from the *Pardess* ("Garden"), the mystical realm of theosophy (see Talmud, tractate of *Haggigah*, p. 14b).

[91] Cf. *O.C.* II, 697–98: "Mais ce qui m'a donné le plus d'éloignement pour les dévots de profession, c'est cette âpreté de moeurs qui les rend insensibles à l'humanité, c'est cet orgueil excessif qui leur fait regarder en pitié le reste du monde. Dans leur élévation sublime, s'ils daignent s'abaisser à quelque acte de bonté, c'est

Julie's aversion toward the devout by profession should guarantee her not imitating them. Moreover, to be perfectly safe, she requests of all her friends including Saint-Preux, as a mark of their friendship toward her, to warn her, should she be on the verge of following the example of those she dislikes so much. Here, too, it seems to us, Julie is eager to please Saint-Preux by stressing her natural aversion toward these devotees and, therefore, the distance that separates her from them, and by making him the judge when to caution her, should he feel that she is slipping. Another lesson she derives from a letter of Milord Edouard, friend of Saint-Preux, is that it is impossible that intolerance should not harden the heart, for how can one treat charitably those one considers damned? Therefore, if we wish to remain human, we should judge not people but their specific deeds and not open so light-heartedly the purgatory to our brothers.

Julie puts an end to her discussion with Saint-Preux by simply writing that she does not wish to argue any more. Rousseau then cuts off the debate which may remain inconclusive theoretically but not practically. For Saint-Preux has modified his stand on prayer, particularly petitionary prayer, in which he sees value for the praying person. Julie, on the other side, will maintain her deistic or rather theistic as well as traditional position on prayer but be on guard against excesses in mystical ecstasies and against resulting intolerance toward humans. She has also proven herself to be not only a *prêcheuse* (preacher) but also a *raisonneuse* (dialectician), as befits an eighteenth-century protagonist who, in addition, is interested in practical implications. Thus, Julie concludes: "Whether I myself am free to have the will to do good or I obtain that will by praying, if in the end I find the means to do good, does it not amount to the same thing? Whether by asking for what I miss I give it to myself or God grants it to me in re-

---

d'une manière si humiliante, ils plaignent les autres d'un ton si cruel, leur justice est si rigoureuse, leur charité est si dure, leur zèle si amer, leur mépris ressemble si fort à la haine, que l'insensibilité même des gens du monde est moins barbare que leur commisération. L'amour de Dieu leur sert d'excuse pour n'aimer personne; ils ne s'aiment pas l'un l'autre. Vit-on jamais d'amitié véritable entre les dévots? Mais plus ils se détachent des hommes, plus ils en exigent; et l'on dirait qu'ils ne s'élèvent à Dieu que pour exercer son autorité sur la terre."

sponse to my prayer, if in order to have it, I must ask for it anyway, why worry about additional explanations?"[92]

Julie has reached the conclusion that arguing just does not help in certain areas. Referring to her husband's case where, she feels, he acts right though, through no fault of his, he does not have the faith, her aim from now on will be "not to convince him but to affect him; it is to show him a captivating example; it is to make religion so attractive to him that he should not be able to resist it . . . [and] compel him to cry out: human nature is of itself incapable of this, something Divine must prevail here.[93]

Julie's wish to convince her husband by example brings to mind that she has been applying this procedure for some time to her children. During Saint-Preux's stay at Clarens, a discussion arose on why she did not teach prayer to her children and she replied: "With regard to prayer, every morning and every night I recite mine aloud in my children's room and that suffices to make them learn it without forcing them to do so."[94] Religion is caught and not taught, someone said. Julie certainly subscribes to this maxim.

G. The Swan Song Prayer of Julie

It is M. de Wolmar who gives Saint-Preux and us a detailed account of the last days of Julie following the illness she had contracted while saving one of her children from drowning. The description mystifies us, takes us by surprise. For we are not used to seeing a dying person have her room rearranged and beautified with pots of flowers and

---

[92]   Ibid., p. 699: "Que je sois libre de vouloir le bien par moi-même, ou que j'obtienne en priant cette volonté, si je trouve enfin le moyen de bien faire, tout cela ne revient-il pas au même? Que je me donne ce qui me manque en le demandant, ou que Dieu l'accorde à ma prière, s'il faut toujours pour l'avoir que je le demande, ai-je besoin d'autre éclaircissement?"

[93]   Ibid., pp. 700–701: "Ce n'est plus de le convaincre, mais de le toucher; c'est de lui montrer un exemple qui l'entraîne, et de lui rendre la religion si aimable qu'il ne puisse lui résister…[et] il sera forcé de se dire: non, l'homme n'est pas ainsi par lui-même, quelque chose de plus qu'humain règne ici."

[94]   Letter III, Part 5, O.C. II, 582–83: "A légard de la prière, tous les matins et tous les soirs je fais la mienne à haute voix dans la chambre de mes enfants, et c'est assez pour qu'ils l'apprennent sans qu'on les y oblige."

then have her family eat dinner in her room and afterwards spend the remaining time with members of her household instead of giving all her attention to her salvation. But then again Julie is not like everybody else. Rousseau made her special.

In her conversations with her pastor, Julie redefines for us the prayer of a dying person: "I prayed in good health, now I resign myself. The prayer of the sick person is patience. Preparation for death is a good life; I do not know any other."[95] She insists on giving what remains of her life to those she has loved and whom it was her duty to take care of. Later, she will be occupied with God alone. She continues by telling us that her conscience is clear and her soul is ready to face the Almighty and, then, bursts into prayer:

> O great Being! Eternal Being, Supreme Intelligence, Source of life and of felicity, Creator, Preserver, Father of man and Ruler of nature, Omnipotent and Very Kind God, of whose existence I never doubted a moment and under whose eyes I have always delighted to live, I know, I rejoice that I am going to appear before Thy throne. In a few days my soul, freed from its trappings, will begin to offer Thee more worthily that immortal homage which should constitute my happiness to all eternity. I regard as nothing all that I shall be up to that moment. My body still lives, but my moral existence is done. I am at the end of my career, and am already judged by the past. To suffer and to die is all that remains for me to do; but this is the way of nature. As for me, I have endeavored to live in such a manner as to have no occasion to concern myself at death, and now that it approaches, I see it come without fear. For one who falls asleep on the bosom of a Father need have no worry about the awakening.[96]

---

[95] Letter XI, Part 6, *O.C.* II, 715: "Je priais en santé; maintenant je me résigne. La prière du malade est la patience. La préparation à la mort est une bonne vie; je n'en connais point d'autre."

[96] Ibid., p. 716: "O grand Etre! Etre éternel, suprême intelligence, source de vie et de félicité, créateur, conservateur, père de l'homme et roi de la nature, Dieu très puissant, très bon, dont je ne doutais jamais un moment, et sous les yeux duquel j'aimais toujours à vivre! Je le sais, je m'en réjouis, je vais paraître devant ton trône. Dans peu de jours mon âme, libre de sa dépouille, commencera de t'offrir plus dignement cet immortel hommage qui doit faire mon bonheur durant l'éternité. Je compte pour rien tout ce que je serai jusqu 'à ce moment. Mon corps vit encore mais ma vie morale est finie. Je suis au bout de ma carrière et déjà jugée sur le passé. Souffrir et mourir est tout ce qui me reste à faire; c'est l'affaire de la nature: Mais, moi, j'ai tâché de vivre de manière à n'avoir pas besoin de

Julie addresses God directly as Father and as Ruler of nature and man. She has utilized ten titles for God, with not a single reference to Christ or any reliance on a mediator, though she claims to have lived and to now die in the Protestant communion which draws its teaching from Holy Writ and (here the eighteenth century pierces through) reason.[97] Her salvation, even at this most serious and solemn occasion of death, is entirely a matter between God and herself. Her deism or rather theism does not falter at this critical juncture. Julie's (and Jean-Jacques') belief in the immortality of the soul is also asserted here. And then the confidence exhibited by Julie (and Jean-Jacques) that they had lived well on this earth and will awaken in the hereafter.

A spiritual concept very dear to Jean-Jacques is that man lives under the gaze of God. In this prayer of Julie, she refers to God "under whose eyes I have always delighted to live." Though to Rousseau, man can find God in the book of nature and within his own conscience, these remain too abstract and impersonal, Grimsley stresses, "until they become part of a living attitude"—man's feeling that God looks upon him. That awareness of the Divine gaze "confers reality upon the living individual." Man's worth also rises as he feels his soul and his being "penetrated by God's look."[98] Julie, therefore, finds bliss in the consciousness that God gazes upon her. Her life has acquired value as God deemed it worthy of being noticed by Him. Again, this recognition and involvement by God also implies a belief in personal Providence, a concept dear to Rousseau, though not to deists such as Voltaire.

In this theistic prayer are conspicuous by their absence any elements characteristic of Christianity, even in its Protestant form. Yet, it finds approval in the sight of the pastor who raises his hands and eyes to heaven and invokes God not in his religion's terms but in Julie's terms in a brief prayer of petition: "Great God! this is the wor-

---

songer à la mort, et maintenant qu'elle approche, je la vois venir sans effroi. Qui s'endort dans le sein d'un père n'est pas en souci du réveil."

[97]   Ibid., p. 714.

[98]   Cf. Grimsley, *Religious Quest*, pp. 107–108.

ship that truly honors Thee; deign to accept it favorably; how seldom do mortals offer Thee the like!"[99]

Perhaps, we thought, it is out of regard for Julie's condition that the pastor offers his prayer in her style. However, what follows does not corroborate this assumption. For, addressing Julie this time, he says: "Madame...I thought I was going to instruct you, but it is you who are teaching me. I have nothing more to say to you. You have the true faith, that which inspires the love of God...."[100] Would Rousseau wish to hint to us here that the pastor, too, is inclined toward some form of deism or theism? Incidentally, it is the pastor who states that Julie is dying a martyr to maternal love.[101]

One more point. The pastor does not hesitate to offer critical comments when he feels they are justified. Thus, when Julie detains him, he, inspired by her example of peace and serenity, complains of the wrong image the public gives to Christianity as the religion for the dying in its convenient belief that fifteen minutes of repentance can efface fifty years of crimes. Moreover, says the pastor, in other cults such as Catholicism, the ceremonial at dying time is more elaborate and instills fear. Whereupon Julie, taking also a partisan stand, responds with an astonishing thanksgiving prayer: "Let us give thanks to Heaven that we have not been born into those venal religions which kill people in order to inherit from them and which, by selling paradise to the rich, carry over into the other world the unjust inequality that reigns in this one here...."[102]

This criticism seems to us to be here an ill-timed reaction against certain practices and not an outright condemnation of Catholicism, as Rousseau's Savoyard Vicar will remain Catholic and Rousseau's general attitude is to encourage people to stay in the religion into which they were born. The ideal of Julie, as of Jean-Jacques, is a middle road

---

[99]   Cf. O.C. II, 717: "Grand Dieu! voilà le culte qui t'honore; daigne t'y rendre propice; les humains t'en offrent peu de pareils."

[100]   Ibid., p. 717: "Madame...je croyais vous instruire, et c'est vous qui m'instruisez. Je n'ai plus rien à vous dire. Vous avez la véritable foi, celle qui fait aimer Dieu...."

[101]   Ibid., p. 717.

[102]   Ibid., p. 718: "Rendons grâces au ciel de n'être point nés dans ces religions vénales qui tuent les gens pour en hériter, et qui, vendant le paradis aux riches, portent jusqu'en l'autre monde l'injuste inégalité qui règne dans celui-ci...."

between impiety and fanaticism—"to be human and pious at the same time."[103] It is also to the ideal of reconciliation of the devotees and the *philosophes*, as symbolized by Julie and M. de Wolmar, that the novel is dedicated.

---

[103]   Ibid., p. 724: "d'être humain et pieux tout à la fois."

CHAPTER VIII

Prayer and its Definition in the *Profession de foi du Vicaire Savoyard*

In 1762, Jean-Jacques published his *Emile ou De L'Education*. As he sees it, a child's life is divided into four periods: infancy, sensation, reason and sentiment. It is only during that fourth and last stage of development, between the ages of fifteen and twenty, that, according to him, religion ought to be introduced. Rousseau does so in the fourth part or book in which is found the *Profession de foi du vicaire savoyard* which caused immediate, considerable upheaval in the political and religious councils, with the result that *Emile* was publicly burned in Paris and Geneva and Pope Clement XIII placed the book on the index. Jean-Jacques himself had to flee Montmorency to escape persecution and arrest ("prise be corps").

Few of Rousseau's contemporaries in a position of power took to heart his statement about the book: "I build more than I destroy."[1] For the originality of the *Profession* resides not in what it discarded of traditional Christianity—that had already been done by others who criticized it severely—but in its reaction against the spreading materialism. In the considered opinion of F. and P. Richard., the *Profession* may have turned away from traditional Christianity some wavering souls but, in return, it brought back to religion many others who were touched by its religiosity. Jean-Jacques thus became the director of conscience of his time, the advisor of those who, though detached

---

[1] "J'établis plus que je ne détruis," letters to Moultou of February 16 and April 25, 1762, quoted by François and Pierre Richard in their introduction to *Emile ou De L'Education* (Paris: Garnier Frères, 1951), p. xx.

from Catholicism, nonetheless had conserved religious needs. It is from this book that also originates the vast, spiritualist movement which, from Bernardin de Saint-Pierre, extends to Chateaubriand, Lamennais, George Sand, Hugo, Renan, Tolstoi.[2] It took the perspective acquired by distance in time to realize that in a century in which religion was embattled, Jean-Jacques "saved of religion what could be saved by conciliating reason with the need to believe."[3]

Precedents in Rousseau

The writing of *Emile* took "twenty years of meditation and three years of work,"[4] Rosseau declared. There were, as F. and P. Richard remind us, a number of partial professions of faith in his life and works before this one which, chronologically, must be looked upon as the end-product of a slow process of maturation. Let us outline them here:[5]

The first traces of Rousseau's profession of faith can be found in an incident related by Mme d'Epinay in her *Mémoires* (I, 380). When the conversation at dinner in the salon of Miss Quinault turned toward atheism, Jean-Jacques stood up and menacingly declared: "As for me, gentlemen, I believe in God.... I will leave the room if you say one more word."[6]

In a *Fragment About God* written, according to Théophile Dufour, in 1735, Jean-Jacques reveals his great earnestness in grappling "with religious problems at the philosophical level."[7] He stresses there the concept of "order" established by God in man and nature and complains that his contemporaries do not follow that order "the principles of which are engraved in the depth of their hearts."[8] The Vicar, too, will stress order in the religious exposition of God.

---

[2]   Ibid, p. xxi.

[3]   Ibid., quoting P. Trahard, p. xxii.

[4]   Ibid., p.xxiii and *Les Confessions*,Book 8, *O.C.* 1, 386.

[5]   Richard, pp. xviii–xix.

[6]   "Et moi, Messieurs, je crois en Dieu.... Je sors si vous dites un mot de plus".

[7]   Cf. Grimsley, *Religious Writings*, p. 8.

[8]   Ibid., p. 8 and *O.C.* IV, 1033.

In his letter of *Advice to a Country Priest* (1752), he exalts the mission of the rural curate, asserts the belief in God to be the basis of morality and diminishes the importance of the catechism.[9]

In an *Allegoric Fragment on Revelation* (1756–57), he speaks of the freedom of the human will and of the fate of three men who tried to enlighten people: the clear-sighted philosopher who is illumined by inner certitude, Socrates whose "wisdom is limited and insufficient to satisfy man's deepest needs" and Jesus who, for Rousseau, "always remains the supreme exponent of the truths of 'natural religion.'"[10]

The *Letter to Voltaire on Providence* (August 18, 1756) in response to his *Poem on the Disaster of Lisbon* defends "God's cause" and criticizes philosophical propaganda as detrimental to serenity and belief.

In the *Letters to Sophie* (31 October, 24 November 1757 and 28 January 1758), he tries to be her director of conscience and F. and P. Richard note on page XIX: "Dogma is sacrificed to conscience and feeling is preferred to everything else."

In the *Letter to D'Alembert on the Theatre* (1758), anticipating *The New Heloisa*, in discussing the supposed Socinianism of the Genevan clergy, he brings forth his own profession of faith, such. as the role of reason in religion, the supremacy of deeds over belief, the high regard in which he holds Scripture.

Finally, the relationship between *The New Heloisa* and the *Profession of Faith of the Savoyard Vicar* has been explicitly acknowledged by Jean-Jacques himself: "One finds in *Emile* the profession of faith of a Catholic priest and in *Héloïse* that of a devout woman. These two works agree sufficiently to enable us to explain one with the help of the other."[11] In his *Confessions*, too, he says: "The profession of faith of

---

9   Grimsley, pp. 25–26, quoting the last part with the reservation that it probably was not included in the original letter.

10 Ibid., p. 80. Since this manuscript has been left by Rosseau without any title, it is also published in *O.C.* IV, with its own suggested title in brackets [Fiction ou morceau allégorique sur la révélation], pp. 1044-54.

11 *Lettres écrites de la montagne*, first letter,-*O.C.* III, 694: "On trouve dans l'*Emile* la profession de foi d'un prêtre catholique et dans l'*Héloïse* celle d'une femme dévote. Ces deux pièces s'accordent assez pour qu'on puisse expliquer l'une par l'autre."

this same dying Julie is exactly the same as that of the Savoyard Vicar."[12]

Thus, gradually and progressively, the religious beliefs have crystallized in Rousseau's mind till they reached full and systematic expression through the *Savoyard Vicar*. Prayer, the language of religion, will be found in the first part of his *Profession de foi* which deals with a positive formulation of "natural religion" or deism. The second part, mostly negative and critical of revealed religion and its practical consequences, is devoid of recourse to prayer.

A. Apostrophizing God in Prayer

The Vicar, spokesman of Rousseau on religion, is, as we know, a combination of two Catholic priests highly regarded by him: the abbé Jean-Claude Gaime whom he knew in Turin in 1728 and the abbé Jean-Baptiste Gâtier whom he had seen in 1729 in the seminary of Annecy. Perched on a high hill with a view of the river Po below, the Alps on the horizon and the rays of the rising sun projecting the shadows of trees and houses on the fields—an ideal setting of natural beauty with which Jean-Jacques always associated religion—the Vicar gave to his young listener and protégé his exposition of a systematic theistic[13] credo.

Utilizing reason as his method, the Vicar had arrived at some basic principles: that there is a will that moves the universe (Aristotle's argument of the Unmoved Mover) and that since matter moves according to laws, a fact which results in order and harmony in nature, it reveals a unique intelligence that established it (cosmological argument). That Being who moves the universe in an orderly way, he calls God. Associated with the concept of God are will, power, intelligence, as well as goodness which is considered a natural resultant. Later, a third principle will be added, namely, that man is free and endowed with an immortal soul. Soon enough, the Vicar becomes

---

[12]   "*Les Confessions*, Book 9, *O.C.*, I., 407: "La profession de foi de cette même Héloïse mourante est exactement la même que celle du vicaire savoyard."

[13]   Cf. *Profession de foi*, Book 4, *O.C.* IV, 606. In the words of the imaginary pupil, Rousseau himself, at the beginning of the second part of this *Profession of Faith*, calls the Vicar's exposition "more or less theism or natural religion."

aware that he has been describing not God Himself but God as He appears in creation. Whereupon, Jean-Jacques makes a most perceptive observation: "I behold God everywhere in His works; I feel Him within me, I see Him all around me; but as soon as I wish to contemplate Him in Himself, as soon as I seek to learn where He is, what He is, what is His essence, He escapes me and my troubled spirit perceives nothing more."[14] This is reminiscent of the Biblical account of the request made by Moses: "Show me, I pray Thee, Thy glory,"[15] which is viewed by Hebrew exegetes as a request to behold God's essence.[16] The Divine reply is that while standing in a cleft of the rock, "thou shalt see My back, but My face shall not be seen,"[17] which is interpreted as meaning seeing God in His works, when He has passed, like seeing the furrows in the water after a boat has passed, but the full essence of God, "the complete revelation of the Divine radiance,"[18] the Bible implies, remains hidden to man. In the words of Sforno: "Not that it is impossible for Me to manifest Myself, but it is impossible for thee to receive the manifestation."[19]

The deeply religious nature of Rousseau's seeking to learn "where He is" can be appreciated better, it seems to us, by juxtaposition with the Jewish *Kedushah*[20] prayer. In it the ministering angels ask one another: "Where is the place of His glory?" meaning: Where is the source of the glory of God that fills the universe?[21] The main stress is

---

[14] Ibid., p. 581: "J'aperçois Dieu partout dans ses oeuvres; je le sens en moi, je le vois tout autour de moi; mais sitôt que je veux le contempler en lui-même, sitôt que je veux chercher où il est, ce qu'il est, quelle est sa substance, il m'échappe et mon esprit troublé n'aperçoit plus rien."

[15] Cf. Exodus, xxxiii. 18.

[16] Commentary by Nachmanides (1194–1270) of Spain on above verse: "He begged to behold the actual Presence in a vision." Commentary by Ibn Ezra (1092–1167) of Spain: "'Thy glory' denotes God Himself."

[17] Cf. Exodus, xxxiii. 23.

[18] Cf. Nachmanides on above verse.

[19] Sforno (1475–1550) of Italy, rabbi, physician and Bible commentator. Commentary on Exodus, xxxiii.20.

[20] This *Kedushah*, the Sanctification of the Divine Name, is recited at attention during the *Mussaf* ("Additional") service on the Sabbath and festivals. It stresses the majestic conception of celestial beings glorifying the Eternal King and asks humans to follow their example.

[21] Elie Munk, *The World of Prayer*, Vol. II (New York: Philipp Feldheim, 1963), p. 56.

on the interrogative pronoun "where." To which the celestial beings above them reply: "Blessed be the glory of the Lord from His abode,"[22] a quotation from the prophet Ezekiel meaning: from His mysterious abode, may He turn in mercy toward His people.

The fact that the essence and source of Divinity challenged and tantalized Rousseau's mind so much that he engaged so extensively in reflection on this subject shows him to be a deep seeker of God and a man of sensitive religious perception. Now, faced with that human predicament and unable to decipher the mysterious riddle, the Vicar (i.e. Rousseau) decides to accept human limitation and stop reasoning on the nature of God, for "a wise man should indulge in them [those reasonings] only with trembling and realize he is not made to fathom them."[23] In their stead, he turns toward creation and particularly man whom he sees as the crown of creation and from his heart rise sentiments of gratitude to the Creator for the many benefits He has bestowed upon man. However, when he turns his closer attention to the various classes of men and to the particular individuals who comprise them, he becomes astonished. For he has seen order, harmony and proportion in the universe, while in the human kind, he witnesses but confusion and disorder. "The elements act in concert, says he, but chaos reigns among men."[24] At this sight, the Vicar apostrophizes God in these words: "O Providence, it is thus that Thou dost govern the world? Beneficent Being, what has become of Thy power? I see evil on this earth."[25]

Meditating thus on human nature, the Vicar explains the presence of evil in the world as a result of the dualism in man. He finds that in man two co-existing forces oppose each other: one lifts up man to moral and intellectual heights and the other pulls him down and enslaves him to his sensual life. Rousseau does not identify these opposing drives within man. In Jewish tradition, however, they have names. They are called respectively the good impulse ("yetzer tov") and the evil impulse ("yetzer ha-ra") and they struggle for the he-

---

[22]   Ezekiel, iii. 12.

[23]   Cf. *O.C.* IV, p.581.

[24]   Ibid., p. 583.

[25]   Ibid., p. 583: "O Providence, est-ce ainsi que tu régis le monde? Etre bienfaisant, qu'est devenu ton pouvoir? Je vois le mal sur la terre."

gemony of man. Rousseau sees in this dualism the guarantee of human freedom of choice as to which to follow. Freedom is thus a distinct and treasured gift of Heaven to man. At the same time, man has the option of abusing the freedom that was given to him and, thereby, bring evil on the world. We certainly cannot impute to God the sins of man. Rousseau extends still further the principle of human freedom and states that, since man is free in his actions, he must be animated by an immaterial substance[26] which is the soul. As for questioning God being a form of prayer, it has ample precedents in the Bible. For instance, when Abraham pleads with God about Sodom and Gomorrah, he does so in the form of questions: "Wilt Thou, indeed, sweep away the righteous with the wicked...? Shall not the Judge of all the earth do justly?"[27] Questioning God is also acceptable in religion. Biblical precedent is one reason. Another reason is that questioning God implies the recognition of the existence of God to whom the questions can be addressed. It also assumes Divine omnipotence, that Providence has the power and the means to improve matters. Finally, it shows that we consider God as just who, therefore, would do no injustice, and hence, when something seems unjust, it may be questioned.

B. Addressing God on Footing of Equality or Conversation With God

To Jean-Jacques, freedom of will is a unique asset of the human being. The Vicar would not want God to take it away from man, even though man often uses this freedom to do evil. For removal of freedom of will would degrade man to the level of the animal acting by instinct. Then, addressing God on a footing of equality, the Vicar prays:

---

[26] Ibid., pp. 586–87.
[27] Genesis, xviii. 23, 25. Another typical example of questioning of God is that of Moses pleading for Divine forgiveness to the people for the sin of the golden calf: "Lord, why doth Thy wrath wax hot against Thy people...? Wherefore, should the Egyptians speak, saying...?" (Exodus, xxxii. 11–12).

"No, God of my soul, I shall never reproach Thee with having made man in Thine image, so that I may be free, good and happy like Thee.[28]

The last two words of this prayer reveal a profoundly individualistic trait of Rousseau's faith and prayer. They express Rousseau's striving to be "like God." This prayer appeared in 1762. As Rousseau got older and came closer to the end of his life, this attitude became clearer and more repeatedly asserted. Thus, in his *Les Rêveries du promeneur solitaire*, published posthumously in the spring of 1782 and believed to have been written in Paris from 1776 to 1778, during the last two years before his death, he will successively aspire to be "impassive like God Himself"[29] and "self-sufficient like God."[30]

The general goal of the religious person is *imitatio Dei*. What it means is that we should imitate the ethical qualities of God and thereby become ethical like our Divine model.[31] However, when Jean-Jacques voices his aspiration to be like God, he does not have in mind the ethical qualities alone. Those seem insufficient to him. What he longs for is to achieve some attributes of the very nature of Divinity, such as absolute self-sufficiency and needing only himself in order to be happy—which implies not needing God Himself any more. Hence, we are here well beyond the religionist's goal of *imitatio Dei*, and certainly not in the realm of the mystic's striving for fusion with God. For Jean-Jacques does not seek to lose himself in God. He wants to be able to do without Him. This is what appears at first sight and with some frequency, and critics have attacked him for it. As François Mauriac writes about Rousseau: "Jean-Jacques never loses sight of himself, and it is at a time when he should seek to forget himself [in prayer], to cease to be, that his attention toward himself redoubles."[32] His feeling of personal existence in this world and in paradise, with

---

[28]   Cf. *O.C.* IV, 587: "Non, Dieu de mon âme, je ne te reprocherai jamais de l'avoir faite à ton image, afin que je puisse être libre, bon et heureux comme toi."

[29]   Cf. *Les Rêveries du promeneur solitaire*, première promenade, *O.C.* I, 999: "impassible comme Dieu même."

[30]   Ibid., cinquième promenade, p. 1047: "on se suffit à soi-même comme Dieu."

[31]   Cf. Talmud, tractate of *Shabbat*, p. 133b: "Be thou like Him: just as He is gracious and compassionate, so be thou gracious and compassionate. "

[32]   François Mauriac, *Trois grands hommes devant Dieu* (Paris: Editions du Capitole, 1930), p. 116.

which he identified happiness, was achieved toward the end of his life when he dreaded death no longer, as he says in the words of his spokesman, the Vicar: "I long for that moment when, relieved of the hindrance of my body, I shall be wholly and consistently *myself* and, to be happy, shall need nothing but my own being."[33] Suffering and persecution made Jean-Jacques still more of a loner, leading him to withdraw within himself and rely on his own inner resources which had to be considerable to satisfy his needs and his bruised ego. As Marcel Raymond put it in his *Notes et Variantes* on the *Rêveries*: "To experience in oneself absolute sufficiency is equivalent to being able to do without God."[34]

This evaluation of Rousseau's striving for self-sufficiency as aiming "to be able to do without God"—it seems to us—goes perhaps a bit too far. It is true that this is the ultimate outcome to which achievement of his wish would lead him. However, the immediate and urgent need for which Jean-Jacques prays is rather a self-sufficiency which would make him ("like God") free and independent of *man* and able to do without his fellow-man. Only the end result of such absolute self-sufficiency would, for all practical purposes, be an ability to do without God too. It sounds unlikely that Rousseau perceived or desired such a result.

Some critics have gone even further. They have seen in Rousseau an aspiration toward self-deification. Thus, Guéhenno feels that Rousseau's conception of sufficiency involves not only being "like God" but rather, he adds, "if not God Himself."[35] Masson in his analysis of the *Savoyard Vicar* finds in this prayer the expression of a pervasive attitude of Jean-Jacques and states: "Almost all the religious meditations of Rousseau end instinctively and more or less consciously in [self] deification."[36] In his *magnum opus*, Masson is more

---

[33] Cf. *La Profession de foi*, O.C. IV, 604–605: "J'aspire au moment où, délivré des entraves de mon corps, je serai moi sans contradiction, sans partage, et n'aurai besoin que de *moi* pour être heureux."

[34] Cf. *Les Rêveries du promeneur solitaire, Notes et Variantes,*" O.C. I,. 1800, note 2: "Eprouver en soi l'absolue suffisance, c'est aussi bien se passer de. Dieu."

[35] Cf. Guéhenno, II, 28.

[36] Jean-Jacques Rousseau, *La Profession de foi du vicaire savoyard*, introduction et commentaire par Pierre-Maurice Masson (Fribourg: Librairie de l'université, 1914), p. 193.

explicit and adds: "In the paradise of Jean-Jacques, God will discreetly efface Himself to make room for Jean-Jacques."[37] In the same vein, Guyot comments: "It is not Jean-Jacques who dissolves himself in God, it is, it seems, on the contrary God Himself who effaces Himself before a deified Rousseau.[38] Finally, in a still more drastic criticism, Masson accuses Rousseau of wanting to supplant God, "to absorb God within himself,"[39] and Guyot quotes this view approvingly.[40]

It seems to us that this criticism is exaggerated. True enough, Rousseau does, indeed, strive to achieve some of God's attributes—self-sufficiency and impassibility leading to happiness without need of anyone besides himself—and in this he is perhaps verging on the sacrilegious. But the really essential attributes of Divinity are omnipotence, omniscience, eternity, ability to create *ex nihilo*, and only if we saw Rousseau striving for any or all of these which describe God's very nature would it be justifiable to say that he strove for self-deification, for supplanting God and the like. To the contrary, we have repeated expressions of his recognition of his human limitations. For example, in the *Rêveries*, he says: "If I had been invisible or omnipotent like God, I would have been beneficent and good like Him."[41] Through his Savoyard Vicar, too, he expresses his inability to fathom God's nature "where He is, what He is, what is His essence."[42] These are pronouncements of a man who knows his place and limitations and does not wish sacrilegiously to exceed them. His aspirations for absolute self-sufficiency, while exceeding the bounds most religionists observe, are then to our mind not so much a reflection of self-aggrandizing presumptuousness, as they are the product of great suffering inflicted on him by people he had had to resort to and depend on. Then why accuse him of striving to supplant God or to have God efface Himself before a deified Rousseau?

---

[37] Cf. Masson, *La Religion de Rousseau*, 11, 120.

[38] Cf. Guyot, p. 38.

[39] Cf. Masson, *La Religion de Rousseau*, II, 120.

[40] Cf. Guyot, p. 38.

[41] Cf. *Rêveries*, sixième promenade, *O.C.* I, 1057.

[42] Cf. *La Profession de foi*, Book 4, *O.C.* IV, 606.

C. Prayer of Adoration and Acceptance of the Divine Decree for the Ultimate Fate of the Wicked

Speaking about the future reward to good people, Jean-Jacques says that the recollection of a virtuous life makes the surviving soul happy, since bliss or misery will result from the very memories of the past life in the soul which is so much more attentive to them when freed from the body. The spirits of those who had been good will enjoy the contemplation of the Supreme Being and the comparison of what they had done with what they ought to have done will yield a corresponding joy in contentment with oneself to the virtuous and regrets to the sinner. Jean-Jacques cannot tell if there will be other sources of happiness or suffering but these are sufficient to console him for this life.[43] For no happiness can exceed that of "existing in accordance with one's own nature."[44] Then, he adds: "This idea [that the good will be compensated for their sufferings] is based less upon the merit of man than upon the notion of goodness which seems to me to be inseparable from the Divine essence."[45] It is a necessary consequence of the assumption that God is consistent with Himself. Here, Jean-Jacques adds a footnote with Scriptural support about God doing things for His own sake. The quotation is from the first verse of Psalm cxv taken, according to Masson,[46] from the Genevan Psalter of 1698. The psalm's Hebrew text reads in its English translation:

> Not unto us, O Lord, not unto us,
> But unto Thy name give glory,
> For Thy mercy and for Thy truth's sake.[47]

The Genevan Psalter has for the third line: "O God, make us revive!" which must have been introduced for purpose of rhyme. The idea

---

[43]   Cf. summary of this difficult passage in Charles W. Hendell, 11, 150.

[44]   Cf. *O.C.* IV, 591.

[45]   Ibid.

[46]   Cf. Masson, *La Profession de foi*, p. 213, note 2, and Grimsley, *Religious Writings*, p. 149, note 4.

[47]   Cf. *O.C.* IV, 591, note:

> Non pas pour nous, non pas pour nous, Seigneur,
> Mais pour ton nom, mais pour ton propre honneur,
>   O Dieu! fais-nous revivre!

itself that God will revive the dead as an act of His own omnipotence and justice is a valid one for the religionist. Rousseau, however, applies it to Divine compensation in the hereafter.

Concerning the sinner's eternal damnation, Jean-Jacques who, in a letter to the Protestant minister of Geneva, Jacob Vernes, dated February 18, 1758, had rejected the concept of eternity of punishment,[48] now speaking as a Vicar, an official of the Church, claims ignorance, though he says he finds it hard to believe that the wicked will be condemned to torments without end, since punishment in their hearts already is meted out in this life. Moreover, pure spirits are without wants and, therefore, their passions and crimes also cease. They can do no more what is not good. Consequently, they cannot be forever miserable. Here, Rousseau's mood changes. He stops giving additional arguments to prove the correctness of his feeling that punishment is not to be eternal and, in their stead, resorts to a prayer of adoration and of acceptance of the Divine decree for the ultimate fate of the wicked:

> O merciful and bounteous Being! whatever Thy decrees may be, I adore them. If Thou punishest the wicked [eternally], I make my feeble reason as nothing before Thy justice; but if, in time, the remorse of these unfortunates shall be blotted out, if their pangs shall end, and if the same peace shall await us all alike one day, I praise Thee for all that. The wicked man, is he not my brother? How often have I been tempted to resemble him! If, delivered from his misery, he lose also the malignity by which it is accompanied, if he is destined to be happy as I myself, then his happiness, far from arousing my jealousy, will only add to my own.[49]

---

[48] Cf. Grimsley, *Religious Writings*, p. 69: 'A l'égard de l'éternité des peines, elle ne saurait s'accorder avec la faiblesse de l'homme ni avec la justice de Dieu, ainsi je la rejette."

[49] Cf. *O.C.* IV, 592: "O Etre clément et bon! quels que soient tes décrets, je les adore; si tu punis [éternellement] les méchants, j'anéantis ma faible raison devant ta justice, mais si les remords de ces infortunés doivent s'éteindre avec le temps, si leurs maux doivent finir, et si la même paix nous attend tous également un jour, je t'en loue. Le méchant n'est-il pas mon frère? Combien de fois j'ai été tenté de lui ressembler! Que, délivré de sa misère, il perde aussi la malignité qui l'accompagne; qu'il soit heureux ainsi que moi: loin d'exciter ma jalousie, son bonheur ne fera qu'ajouter au mien."

René Pomeau, commenting on prayers of adoration, states: "Distance drives man to adoration which is nothing else but the awareness of this distance."[50] Deists were particularly conscious of Divine majesty and, therefore, distance. Theists were so to a lesser extent, since they maintained a balance between transcendence and immanence. The Vicar, in his exposition in our prayer, acknowledges Divine superiority over his "feeble reason" and declines to take a personal stand on the painful issue of the suffering of the wicked. Rather does he look up to Divinity for guidance, submitting to His decision if it be positive, and praising God if it be negative, assuring Him in the process that he will not mind it if punishment of the wicked be reduced or cancelled due, obviously, to Divine forgiveness.

Deserving of note here are the striking similarities in ideas between this prayer by the Vicar and the views followed in a prayer by Julie, though they end up with different conclusions. Julie has said: "The God that I serve is a merciful God, a Father: what moves me most is His goodness; that surpasses in my eyes all His other attributes; it is the only one that I really perceive…since He is just, He is merciful. The vengeful God is the God of the wicked; I can neither fear Him for myself nor beseech Him against someone else. O God of peace, God of goodness, it is Thee that I adore.…"[51] We analyzed this declaration of Julie when we studied her prayer in *La Nouvelle Héloïse*. In comparing it with the Vicar's prayer, we find that both deal with the adoration theme. Both appeal to Divine clemency and goodness, and stress Divine justice which makes for Divine clemency, since God knows man to be weak and subject to temptation. Both shun Divine strictness and severity, and hope that it is clemency that will prevail. Both also rely on expressed or assumed remorse. The difference lies in the fact that the Vicar says explicitly that he will submit to the Divine decision on the eternity of punishment of the wicked, while Julie re-

---

[50]   Cf. Pomeau, *La Religion de Voltaire*, p. 423: "La distance réduit l'homme à l'adoration qui n'est rien d'autre que le sentiment de cette distance."

[51]   Cf. *La Nouvelle Héloise*, Part 6, letter 8, *O.C.* II, 696: "Le Dieu que je sers est un Dieu clément, un père: ce qui me touche est sa bonté; elle efface à mes yeux tous ses autres attributs; elle est le seul que je conçois…puisqu'il est juste, il est clément. Le Dieu vengeur est le Dieu des méchants; je ne puis ni le craindre pour moi, ni l'implorer contre un autre. O Dieu de paix, Dieu de bonté, c'est toi que j'adore.…"

bels against a "God of retribution" and seems to accept God on her terms only.

Concerning the Vicar's own attitude toward reason, a dual attitude is apparent. In our prayer, he says: "I make my feeble reason as nothing before Thy justice." In the next prayer, we find him again saying: "The worthiest use I can make of my reason is to deem myself as naught in Thy presence."[52] Yet, in the second part of the *Profession of Faith*, the Vicar states: "It is vain to tell me: subdue your reason...I must have reasons to subdue my reason."[53] And further: "To tell me to subdue my reason is to outrage its author."[54] One answer might perhaps be that when the Vicar addresses God, he is willing to admit that human reason has its limitations, that it cannot fathom Divine nature and, hence, many Divine decisions, too, are beyond its ken and are part of the Incomprehensible.[55] However, when discussing religion with human beings, he expects them to justify their position and not to invoke blind faith for lack of a good justification. In other words, the Vicar makes a distinction between matters concerning the Divine that are inherently beyond human comprehension and matters which he regards as comprehensible and subject to acceptance or rejection in accordance with human reason. A good reason to subdue his reason would probably be a demonstration that the subject under discussion belongs in the category of the incomprehensible.

D. Prayer of Self-Humbling, Finite Man Before Infinite God

The Vicar returns to the discussion of God's essence and realizes that it strains his mind in vain since it does not yield any clear notions. He then moves on to the concept of creation *ex nihilo* with no greater success, for "The idea of creation confuses me and goes beyond my

---

[52] Cf. *La Profession de foi*, O.C. IV, 594: "Le plus digne usage de ma raison est de s'anéantir devant toi."

[53] Ibid., p. 610: "Ils ont beau me crier, soumets ta raison...il me faut des raisons pour soumettre ma raison."

[54] Ibid., p. 614: "Me dire de soumettre ma raison, c'est outrager son auteur."

[55] Ibid., p. 628: "Je tâche d'anéantir ma raison devant la suprême intelligence."

reach."[56] His mind cannot fathom the concept of God's eternity either. What it does conceive is that God was in the past, is in the present and will still be in the future, even if everything were to end one day.[57] Having reached this insurmountable difficulty Rousseau, before

---

[56] Cf. *Profession de foi*, *O.C.*, IV, 593: " L'idée de création me confond et passe ma portée." One year later, in 1763, in his *Lettre à Christophe de Beaumont*, archbishop of Paris, Jean-Jacques returns to the idea of creation *ex nihilo* which he has difficulty in accepting and toward which the Vicar maintains a respectful doubt, and tries to blame this problem on possibly faulty translations of the Bible. For support of his view, Rousseau mentions the authority of a M. de Beausobre who is supposed to have proven that "the notion of creation [*ex nihilo*] is not to be found in the ancient Judaic theology" (see *O.C.* IV, 957). Grimsley, too, brings in a footnote the text of a 1782 edition of Rousseau's *Mélanges* in which Jean-Jacques says: "The Hebrew word which was translated by *create, make something out of nothing* means *to make, to produce something with magnificence*. Rivet even claims that neither this Hebrew word *bara*, nor the corresponding Greek word, nor even the Latin word *creare*, can be restricted to the particular meaning of producing something out of nothing..." (see *Religious Writings*, p. 261). In response to Rousseau's solution of his difficulty, we must state that the "Judaic theology" on the authority of which M. de Beausobre invokes the denial of the nature of *creatio ex nihilo* DOES precisely regard the Hebrew word *bara* as creation out of nothing. In fact, this is one of the cardinal principles of the Jewish faith. It is rather the word *yatzar* which has the meaning of shaping, fashioning, giving form to pre-existent material. In English, French and Latin, the word "create" ("*créer*" and "*creare*") is, indeed, not restricted to the particular meaning of producing something out of nothing, as Rivet says. It has both the meanings of *bara* and *yatzar*. However, contrary to Rivet's claim, the Hebrew bara does, we repeat, specifically mean *creatio ex nihilo*. Rousseau might have had less difficulty with a concept of creation presented by Nachmanides (1194–1270) born in Spain and also known as Ramban (formed by initials of *Rabbi Moshe ben Nachman*) who wrote that "everything that exists under the sun or above it was not made from non-existence at the outset." Rather, he says, God brought forth out of nothing an intangible, ethereal substance having the potential of becoming tangible and assuming form. "This was the primordial matter created by God," after which, says Ramban, "He did not create [*bara*] anything but formed [*yatzar*] and made things from it." (See Ramban, *Commentary on the Torah*, book of Genesis, translation and annotation by Charles B. Chavel [New York: Shilo Publishing House, 1971], p. 23.)

[57] Cf. *Profession de foi*, *O.C.* IV, 593: "Ce que je conçois, c'est qu'il est avant les choses, qu'il sera tant qu'elles subsisteront, et qu'il serait même au-delà, si tout devait finir un jour." This is reminiscent of the most popular Hebrew hymn of trust in God who is the highest and at the same time the nearest, *Adon Olam*

he proceeds to discuss the moral consequences of his analysis of Divinity and man's inner life, concludes this part of his exposition with the following summary and prayer: "In short, the more I strive to contemplate His infinite essence, the less do I comprehend it. But He exists and that is sufficient for me. The less I comprehend Him, the more I adore Him. I humble myself and say to Him: 'Being of beings, I am because Thou art. To meditate ceaselessly on Thee is to raise myself to my real source. The worthiest use I can make of my reason is to deem myself as naught in Thy presence: it is rapture to my soul, it is the delight of my weakness, to feel myself overwhelmed by Thy greatness.'"[58]

This prayer strikes an anti-intellectual or rather a supra-intellectual note. Masson calls it an "act of intellectual humility"[59] which he contrasts with later rationalistic assertions by the Vicar. As we said before, there is not necessarily a contradiction between them.

("Eternal God"). This hymn opens and closes the Jewish morning worship and is recited at night before one lies down to rest. It is attributed to the renowned Jewish poet and philosopher, Solomon Ibn Gabirol (called by the poet Heinrich Heine the "Nightingale of Piety") who lived in eleventh-century Spain. In this hymn, we find the following lines:

> And at the end, when all shall cease to be,
> The revered God alone shall still be King.
> He was, He is, and He shall be
> In glorious eternity.

Its universal appeal has been described by the Russo-British bacteriologist, Waldemar M. Haffkine: "Every fresh discovery confirms the fact that in all Nature's infinite variety there is one single Principle at work, One Power that is of no beginning and no end; that has existed before all things were formed, and will remain when all is gone; the Source and Origin of all, and yet in Itself beyond any conception or image that man can form." (See Joseph H. Hertz, *The Authorized Daily Prayer Book*, revised edition [New York: Bloch Publishing Company, 1948], p. 8.)

[58] Ibid., p. 594: "Enfin, plus je m'efforce de contempler son essence infinie, moins je la conçois; mais elle est, cela me suffit; moins je la conçois, plus je l'adore. Je m'humilie, et lui dis: 'Etre des êtres, je suis parce que tu es; c'est m'élever à ma source que de te méditer sans cesse. Le plus digne usage de ma raison est de s'anéantir devant toi: c'est mon ravissement d'esprit, c'est le charme de ma faiblesse, de me sentir accablé de ta grandeur.'"

[59] Cf. Masson, *La Profession de foi*, p. 229.

Bergson defines the Christian mystic and, we think, the same applies to any mystic, as one who is convinced that, as a result of a supra-intellectual experience, his soul has entered into direct communication with God, the transcendental principle of all life.[60] Jean-Jacques does not accept what is contrary to reason but only what is above and beyond it. The Vicar has struggled with the problem of the essence of God. His reason, he had to admit, could lead him no further. Proceeding then above reason, the Vicar may just have made the leap into mystical communion with Divinity, which evokes in him his humility, a desire to fuse with Divinity and a cry of adoration.

Jean-Jacques attached great importance to this prayer and quotes it *in toto* as well as the two paragraphs preceding it in his letter to M. de Baumont[61] who, on August 20, 1762, had issued a *Mandement* condemning *Emile* as heresy. Rousseau's reply, completed in mid-November 1762 and published in March 1763, refutes, among others, the prelate's accusation against him that he is self-contradictory in claiming at the same time that he does not know God's nature and yet describes Divine attributes. In his defense, Rousseau quotes his own writing in the Vicar, namely, the two paragraphs preceding the prayer and the prayer itself.

Interestingly, Voltaire wrote on the margin of the paragraph containing this prayer "Très beau" and, if it pleased Voltaire so much, we are not surprised that the archbishop felt that Rousseau's book was deficient in Christian dogmas. For Voltaire admired more than the beauty of the literary style.

On the other hand, there is a work written by the abbé Feller in 1773 and entitled *Philosophical Catechism*. Utilizing the traditional format of such works in questions and answers, he asks: "What advantages does the Christian derive from his faith in the mysteries of his religion?" In the answer, he avers that the incomprehensibility of the nature of God and all ideas and feelings we have about Divinity are confirmed by the "obscurity of the mysteries." For a God whose nature and works had only what our feeble reason could understand would, indeed, be an imperfect and limited Deity. The abbé then quotes Saint-Augustine to the effect that we know God only by our

---

[60]　Cf. F.C. Green, p. 254.

[61]　Cf. *Letter to M. de Beaumont*, O.C. IV, 958–59.

inability to comprehend Him. After quoting Saint Leo, i.e. Pope Leo I also, the abbé adds that philosophers have talked on this matter like the saints and then proceeds to quote Rousseau,[62] giving the complete paragraph with the prayer which we have just analyzed.

Needless to stress that Jean-Jacques has never defined the incomprehensibility of Divine essence in terms of the dogmas which Christianity regards as mysteries. As Grimsley put it succinctly: "Although he [Rousseau] calls himself a 'Christian,' he clearly has no sympathy for such typical Christian doctrines as the Incarnation, original sin and grace.[63] Still, the quote by the abbé, eleven years after the book was banned, put on the index and attacked by the Paris archbishop, shows that religionists felt there was some positive religious content in this book worth knowing.

E. The Vicar's Definition of Prayer and A Prayer of Adoration Including Part of the "Pater"

The Vicar aspires to the moment when he is freed of the hindrance of the body and needs only himself to be happy. In the meantime, by disregarding all his ills, he draws happiness in this world from contemplation. The Vicar tells us what he does and, in the process, gives us his definition of prayer. He completes it with a prayer of adoration which includes part of the *Pater*:

> To raise myself in advance as much as possible to that state of happiness, strength and liberty, I practice sublime contemplation. I meditate upon the order of the universe, not to explain it by presumptuous systems, but to admire it unceasingly, to worship the wise Creator who reveals Himself through it. I converse with Him, I let His Divine essence permeate all my faculties; I am moved by His kindness, I bless Him for His gifts, but I do not ask Him for anything (or, as his contemporaries understood: I do not pray to

---

62 Abbé François-Xavier de Feller (1735–1802) wrote under the pseudonym of Flexier de Réval, *Catéchisme philosophique ou Recueil d'observations propres à défendre la religion chrétienne contre ses ennemis* (Lyon: Chez Périsse frères, Libraires, Paris: Au dépôt de la librairie de Périsse Frères, first edition 1773. We have used 1830 edition), III, 12–13,.

63 Cf. Grimsley, *Religious Writings*, p. 215.

Him). What should I ask of Him? That He should change for me the course of things, that He should perform miracles on my behalf? I who must love above all else the order established by His wisdom and maintained by His Providence, should I then wish that order to be upset for me? No, such a rash wish should merit being punished rather than granted. Neither do I ask of Him the power to do good: why ask of Him what He has given me? Has He not granted me a conscience so that I might love the good, reason so that I might learn to recognize it, freedom so that I might choose it? If I do evil, I have no excuse; I do it because I wish it. To ask Him to change my will is tantamount to asking of Him what He asks of me; it is tantamount to wanting Him to do my work while I garner the rewards of it. Not to be satisfied with my state is to wish no longer to be a man, it is to wish something other than what is, it is to wish disorder and evil. Source of justice and truth, merciful and kind God! In my confidence in Thee, the supreme wish of my heart is that Thy will be done. Making my will join Thine, I do what Thou doest, I comply with Thy goodness; it seems to me that thus I partake in advance of the supreme happiness which is the reward of doing so.[64]

Guyot considers this entire passage, and not only its ending, as a prayer.[65] The tone certainly has the flavor of prayer, with a needed

---

[64]   Cf. *Profession de foi*, O.C. IV, 605: "Pour m'élever d'avance autant qu'il se peut à cet état de bonheur, de force et de liberté, je m'exerce aux sublimes contemplations. Je médite sur l'ordre de l'univers, non pour l'expliquer par de vains systèmes, mais pour l'admirer sans cesse, pour adorer le sage auteur qui s'y fait sentir. Je converse avec lui, je pénètre toutes mes facultés de sa divine essence; je m'attendris à ses bienfaits, je le bénis de ses dons; mais je ne le prie pas. Que lui demanderais-je? qu'il changeât pour moi le cours des choses, qu'il fît des miracles en ma faveur? Moi qui dois aimer pardessus tout l'ordre établi par sa sagesse et maintenu par sa providence, voudrais-je que cet ordre fût troublé pour moi? Non, ce voeu téméraire mériterait d'être plutôt puni qu'exaucé. Je ne lui demande pas non plus le pouvoir de bien faire: pourquoi lui demander ce qu'il m'a donné? Ne m'a-t-il pas donné la conscience pour aimer le bien, la raison pour le connaître, la liberté pour le choisir. Si je fais le mal, je n'ai point d'excuse; je le fais parce que je le veux: lui demander de changer ma volonté, c'est lui demander ce qu'il me demande; c'est vouloir qu'il fasse mon oeuvre et que j'en recueille le salaire; n'être pas content de mon état, c'est ne vouloir plus être homme, c'est vouloir autre chose que ce qui est, c'est vouloir le désordre et le mal. Source de justice et de vérité, Dieu clément et bon! dans ma confiance en toi, le suprême voeu de mon coeur est que ta volonté soit faite. En y joignant la mienne, je fais ce que tu fais, j'acquiesce à ta bonté; je crois partager d'avance la suprême félicité qui en est le prix."

[65]   Cf. Guyot, p.35.

minor change of the pronouns from the third to the second person singular. Be that a prayer or a statement, we do have here the Vicar's conception of prayer and it calls for analysis and consideration.

The single sentence in this entire text which was most striking to Rousseau's contemporaries is the assertion "Je ne le prie pas." Jean-Jacques was vehemently attacked for it because it was taken to mean: "I do not pray to Him." Yet, when we read it in its context: "...je le bénis de ses dons; mais je ne le prie pas. Que lui demanderais-je?," it seems clear that its correct meaning is: "...I bless Him for His gifts; but I do not ask Him for anything. What should I ask of Him?" In French, the word "prier" is used equally often for both "to pray to God" and "to ask" or "to request." Jean-Jacques used it in the second sense, as evidenced by its being followed immediately by "Que lui demanderais-je?" as a synonym to "prier." When we examine this sentence in conjunction with the text preceding it, "I meditate upon the order of the universe...to worship the wise Creator...I converse with Him, I let His Divine essence permeate all my faculties; I am moved by His kindness, I bless Him for His gifts, but I do not ask Him for anything. What should I ask of Him?," we see that the Vicar rather clearly means to say that he addresses to God prayers of adoration and thanks but he does not *petition* Him.

Still, the sentence was taken to be a rejection of all prayer, and none other than Vernes, Genevan minister and former friend of Rousseau, took him to task for it. This interpretation of the phrase was also of crucial importance in the condemnation of Rousseau and his work by the City Council of Geneva. Strong protests against this condemnation were voiced in the city to which the powerful *procureur-général* gave a formal reply and, additionally, justified the city's condemnation of Rousseau in his. (i.e. Tronchin's) anonymously published *Letters Written from the Countryside* (*Lettres écrites de la campagne*) in August of 1763. Rousseau now had to defend himself and justify his religious views, particularly those expressed in the *Savoyard Vicar*. He did so, at the instigation of Genevans who had protested the unjust treatment afforded Rousseau and his work, in his *Letters Written from the Mountain* (*Lettres écrites de la montagne*) published in December 1764. In the Third Letter, he refers specifically to the accusation that he "rejects prayer"[66] by pointing out the presence of a prayer beginning with the words "Source of justice and truth" in the very passage which was attacked. In that same letter, while pursuing his defense, he amplifies his views which were expressed indirectly by his spokesman, the Vicar, by adding: "It is true that he [the Vicar] does not believe that it is absolutely necessary to ask of God anything in particular; yet, he does not disapprove of those who wish to do so [to make specific requests]." The second half of this statement by Rousseau is important to us because, from the long talk of the Vicar, it is not clear whether he does or does not tolerate in others prayers of petition. As for himself, he, the Vicar, does not resort to these prayers, since he is convinced that God is a good Father who knows better than His children what is good for them. Jean-Jacques then enumerates what he considers justified kinds of prayer: homage, adoration, praise, contemplation of Divine greatness, avowal of our nothingness, resignation to His will, submission to His laws, a pure and holy life. He finds support for his view in Scripture where, he says, the word "prayer" is often used in the sense of homage or adoration. And then, he emphasizes again, but this time in his own name and not the Vicar's, that: "As for myself, I reject none of the ways of honoring God. I have always approved of joining a church where prayers are offered to Him. I do so. The Savoyard Vicar himself did so too."[67]

We have here in essence the same attitude as that of Saint-Preux who, though not advocating petitionary prayer, is tolerant of those who address such prayers to Divinity, with the reservation, though, that it is we who grant our requests to ourselves and not God. However, in the text of this Third Letter, Rousseau, talking directly for himself, makes no such reservation and, perhaps because he is on the defensive, limits himself to stressing that he personally "rejects none" of the forms of prayer and the Vicar "does not disapprove" of those who wish to make requests of God, though, as we have just seen, Rousseau's predilection is for prayers of praise and adoration. Jean-Jacques also recommends joining a Church, possibly because he sees special value in communal worship.

---

[66]   Cf. *Lettres écrites de la montagne, Troisième Lettre,* O.C. III, 751.
[67]   Ibid., pp. 751–52.

With these amplifications in mind, let us return to the Vicar's ex-position. We shall follow closely its structure as outlined by Gouhier.[68] The Vicar aspires to that "state of happiness, strength and liberty" which will be the state of the soul liberated of the body and of society. He says: "I practice sublime contemplation." What are those exercises and practices? They are meditations which consist less in understand-ing rationally the order of the universe than in providing the heart with motives of exaltation: "I meditate upon the order of the universe, not to explain it by presumptuous systems, but to admire it unceas-ingly, to worship the wise Creator who reveals Himself through it." This adoration is accompanied by gratitude: "I am moved by His kindness, I bless Him for His gifts." However, he does not solicit them: "I do not ask of Him anything" (or, as understood by his con-temporaries, "I do not pray to Him," says the Vicar, using the word "pray" as synonymous with "request" or "petition"). For: "What should I ask of Him?" Two types of requests present themselves to him and he will reject them both. One is "that He should change for me the course of things, that He should perform miracles on my be-half." With a Malebranchist reply, he denounces the impiety of such a possibility: "I who must love above all else the order established by His wisdom…should I then wish that order to be upset for me? No, such a rash wish should merit being punished rather than granted." The second possibility concerns requests for God's help in our inner struggles: should I "ask of Him the power to be good?" The Vicar's answer is: "Why ask of Him what He has given me? Has He not granted me a conscience so that I might love the good, reason so that I might learn to recognize it, freedom so that might choose it?" This phrase is almost a verbatim transcript of Saint-Preux's letter to Julie.[69] The difference between them, in our opinion, is that Saint-Preux feels that with the faculties bestowed on us by God, we give to ourselves what we ask for, as we raise ourselves to God in prayer. The Vicar, on the other hand, could seem to the reader to be doing away with any and all prayers of petition, even those requesting moral, emotional or inspirational support, were it not for Rousseau's Third Letter in which he elaborates on the Vicar's views and informs us that the

---

[68] Cf. pp. 120–21.
[69] Cf. *La Nouvelle Héloïse*, Part 6, letter 7, O.C. II, 683.

Vicar "does not disapprove" of such prayers by those who wish to offer them. He just does not resort to them himself. Gouhier points out that the Vicar does not even mention a third possible type of request, a request for grace and salvation. Having thus dismissed both kinds of petitionary prayer (which he presented in his rhetorical questions) as unjustified, the Vicar ends his analysis with a prayer of adoration, the core of which is a phrase from the first part of the Pater: "Source of justice and truth.... 'Thy will be done'...."

In the Third Letter of the *Letters Written from the Mountain* where Jean-Jacques explains, defends and clarifies the position of the Vicar on prayer, he quotes in a footnote Matthew xxvi.39: "Not what I want, but what Thou wanteth," and adds: "This is the Dominical Prayer itself. It is completely contained in these words: 'Thy will be done.' Any other prayer is superfluous and only contradicts this one."[70] In other words, the expression of complete submission of our desires and will to those of God are, in Rousseau's view, the essence of prayer. The Vicar's prayer, his wish to "join his will to God's will," is the embodiment of this view, and Rousseau's addition that any other prayer is "superfluous" or "contradictory to this one" injects the note that perhaps the expression of submission of that part of the *Pater* is actually the *only* kind of prayer man is really entitled to offer to God.

Burgelin reminds us that the Vicar refers in his prayer neither to God's pardon nor to sin but only to submission as worded in the Dominical prayer. It was not so in Rousseau's youth in his two great prayers at Les Charmettes. Then, in the first prayer, he had insisted on the nothingness of man: "We are but dust and ashes before Thee, and it is only with trembling that we should appear before Thy dreaded presence, but Thou hast yet more mercy than majesty." He thanks God for having created us and implores His grace to lead us on the path of virtue. The second still mentioned: "Pardon the sins I have committed."[71] But later, throughout his theistic prayers, these concepts do not appear any more. The closest he comes to Christian prayer forms is in the stress of this one part of the *Pater* "Thy will be done," but he eliminates the requests for daily bread, for pardon, as

---

70   Cf. *Lettres écrites de la montagne, Troisième lettre*, O.C. III, 752, note.
71   Burgelin, *La Philosophie de l'existence*, p. 462.

well as the use of the formula of the Trinity—all of which are conspicuous by their absence.

The vicar addresses a prayer of adoration to the "Source of justice and truth, merciful and kind God" with whom he says he converses. Saint-Preux offers no prayer at all, neither one composed by him nor one which is part of a religious tradition. He thinks God does not answer (or even listen to?) prayer and if one prays expecting God to answer and help, it is a vain hope. The Vicar, on the other hand, feels one ought not to petition God because He has already provided us with everything but *not* because He would not answer. As summed up by the critic of the Pléiade edition of Rousseau's writings: the Vicar's God with whom one can converse at least is, indeed, more personal than the God of Saint-Preux.[72]

---

[72] Cf. *Emile ou De l'éducation, Notes et Variantes*, O.C. IV, 1568, note 2.

CHAPTER IX

Criticism of Opposition to Petitionary Prayer

Rousseau—Theist Rather Than Deist

As we have seen in letters six, seven and eight in the sixth part of *La Nouvelle Héloïse* and in the discussion of prayer by the Vicar in *Profession de foi* (notably page 605), the admissibility of prayers of request, of petition, is an issue in Rousseau's conception of prayer. Such prayers are generally opposed and at best tolerated by Saint-Preux and the Savoyard Vicar. This attitude is not uniquely Rousseau's. The problem is universal and religions which do accept petitionary prayers have had to deal with it.

At the outset, let us state that petition or request has played such a central role in religion that by metonymy—use of one word for another that it suggests—prayer has often been identified with asking something from God, with request. True enough, it is this too, but it is not only this. Adoration, praise, submission are also expressed in prayer, and Rousseau offers such prayers without reservation, regarding them as morally uplifting and unquestionably valuable. Let us then present what is in general the problem of prayer and subsequently what is considered as the special problem of petitionary prayer, and try to offer some answers. We have selected as references Kant's attitude to prayer and the Jewish response to this universal problem as it appears in the religious literature of Judaism as well as in the writings of the Jewish classic authority in this field, the Spanish-Jewish religious philosopher Joseph Albo (1380–1440), author of the *Book of Principles*, and in an essay on prayer by the contemporary American-Jewish scholar and philosopher, Dr. Eliezer Berkovits.

To deistic thinking, as a general rule, God has created the world, established the laws by which it is functioning and returned or retreated to His transcendence, maintaining no more contact with creation. In such an outlook, God is distant, unapproachable, and prayer is well-nigh pointless. No wonder that many deists have strenuously objected to prayers of request. They do accept, though, prayers of adoration and submission. However, they probably regard such prayers only as expressions of man's intellectual perception of the greatness of the Creator. Their value, too, would be not so much moral as intellectual and perhaps esthetic—similar to the value of poetry expressing man's perception of and reaction to beauty. There were those who could not look on prayers as having any moral value, since in their view everything in the world, including every man's nature and actions, is completely determined. This point is forcefully developed by Dr. Berkovits who feels that, by the same reasoning, prayers of adoration and of submission should also be rejected. He writes: "If all things have been 'ordered, foreseen and linked together in a chain from the beginning,'[1] if one is part of a cosmos which is ruled by impersonal and unbreakable universal laws, even submission has little moral and spiritual value. Only where there is freedom to rebel is submission a decision and a deed. To submit in a deterministic universe is simply not being a fool. If one pursued the thought to its ultimate consequences, one would have to say that in such a universe there is indeed nothing else left to man but to submit, and this not only when he feels inclined to pray but also when it comes to human activity of any kind. Ethical activity [in particular] requires an area of freedom where man may choose and decide in personal responsibility. Ethical action is only possible in a world in which all things are not ordered and linked together in a chain from the beginning."[2] The completely deterministic view of the world when followed to its logical conclusions excludes, then, not only any moral value from prayer but also from ethics and actually precludes man's very ability to choose to act ethically. Only theistic   religion   which

---

[1] This is a quote from Voltaire's prayer in the *Sermon des cinquante* listed in Peter Gay, *Deism: An Anthology*, p. 145.

[2] Eliezer Berkovits, *Studies in Torah Judaism—Prayer* (New York: Yshiva University Department on Special Publications, 1962), pp. 73–74.

posits that God has endowed man with free will to make an ethical and religious choice, and that it matters to God how each man utilizes this freedom, it appears then, can ascribe moral value to choosing right and to choosing to submit to God. (And, we might add in parentheses, such a God, in turn, is close enough to be petitioned as well as adored, and interested enough in the nature and the actions of the petitioning individual to grant the request when He sees fit.)

While to inflexible deists, as we just said, prayers could have no moral value, Immanuel Kant (1724–1804), a contemporary and an admirer of Rousseau, at the end of his book entitled *Religion Within the Limits of Reason Alone*, presents a view of non-petitionary prayer which DOES have moral value because man is regarded as having free will and thus moral responsibility and ability to improve his moral disposition. He considers the common attitude toward the value and purpose of prayer as an alleged and not a real service of God and formulates his own idealized view of its purpose and value.

To Kant, the "*spirit* [i.e. the essence] *of prayer*" is "a heart-felt wish to be well-pleasing to God in our every action and abstention," a disposition to discharge the duties to which we are obligated by "commands of God." This wish "should be present in us 'without ceasing' (I Thessalonians V, 17)."[3] It is this heart-felt wish, this disposition, that has real importance and moral value. Actual prayer is, or should be, only a verbalized expression of this inner wish, its statement in words. Only the wish, the "spirit of prayer" as defined above, is important and can be regarded as a duty of man. Verbalized prayer, the "letter of prayer," is to Kant of secondary value, being viewed by him as only a *means* to quickening within man that desirable inner disposition or wish. The mere pronouncing of the words of the prayer cannot gain Divine approval. Prayer to Kant, then, is important insofar as it affects positively the praying individual himself. As for God, He will be pleased not by the prayer itself but by its ensuing effect on the one who is praying, if indeed it has produced in him a desirable effect, an inner betterment.

---

[3]   Immanuel Kant, *Religion Within the Limits of Reason Alone*, translated with introduction and notes by Theodore M. Greene and Hoyt H. Hudson (La Salle, Illinois: The Open Court Publishing Co., first publication 1934, reprinted New York: Harper and Brothers, 1960), p. 183.

The highest form of prayer to Kant, as to Rousseau and the psalmists (not to mention the mystics) is, therefore, wordless. It is a continuous *inner* "devotion." By the same token, contemplation which "transports the mind into that sinking mood called *adoration* is...so soul-elevating a power that words...must needs pass away as empty sound because the emotion arising from such a vision of the hand of God is inexpressible."[4] Yet, most people and certainly children cannot reach the heights of wordless prayer. Therefore, "it is...necessary carefully to inculcate set forms of prayer in children (who still stand in need of the letter [of prayer], even in their earliest years," but do so in such a way that they learn that saying the words has no value in itself, that the words are used "merely to, quicken the disposition to a course of life well-pleasing to God."[5] This is so important to Kant because he, like other critics of religion and prayer, sees the main problem of prayer *as commonly practiced* in its being considered as an end in itself, supposedly venerating God by verbal glorifications but without a corresponding inner feeling or striving toward moral self-improvement. This, to be sure, is also the truly desirable attitude toward prayer taught by theistic religion.

In summary, prayers of devotion and adoration are acceptable to Kant and even advocated by him as a means by which man seeks to improve his moral disposition through his own effort and not through supernatural help. The seeking of this improvement and not the prayer *per se* is well-pleasing to God and has a positive moral value.

Kant's attitude toward prayers of petition, on the other hand, is strongly negative. He considers them as an attempt "to divert God (to our present advantage) from the plan of His wisdom...through the persistent importunity of one's request.[6] In Kant's view, prayers of request are an endeavor to make God change. His will and, as such, they are not only devoid of moral value but actually reprehensible. He even regards as unworthy those requests, the object of which is "indeed moral, but yet possible only through supernatural influence (or at least awaited by us from this source alone because we do not

---

4   Ibid., pp. 185–86.
5   Ibid., p. 186.
6   Ibid., p. 184.

wish to trouble ourselves to bring it about—as, for example, the change of heart…)."[7]

As we see, Kant distinguishes between requests for concrete needs, such as the daily bread, and requests for spiritual improvement through supernatural influence which some might consider to be more worthy; but he disapproves of both. In discussing Saint-Preux's attitude toward petitionary prayer (Chapter VII, Section E above), we have made a similar distinction between requests for moral and spiritual strength, the only kind Saint-Preux and Julie discuss, and requests for concrete benefits. Saint-Preux does not disapprove of prayers of request for moral strength but believes that whatever effect they may have does not come from on high but rather from within the praying individual himself. In this, he comes through as believing in God's responsiveness as much as Kant does, for, according to Kant, one should not importune the Divine Being to do so. On the contrary, we should strengthen our moral disposition only through personal effort.

Interestingly and obviously to us, the Sages of Judaism in Talmud and *Midrash* were also conscious of the fact that prayer might be regarded as an imposition on God. Nonetheless, they found prayer possible and proper precisely because, in the Judaic conception of God and man, God desires to be imposed upon by man. Dr. Berkovits backs up this view by quotations from the *Midrash* which states: "A human being may have a patron whom he approaches for assistance. If he will trouble him too much, the patron will cease supporting him. God is not like this; but the more a person beseeches Him with his needs and requests, the more God loves him."[8] The fact that, by comparison with Divine wisdom and grandeur what man wants of God appears so insignificant and trivial, is no deterrent to approaching God. On the contrary, man's insignificance and insufficiency are the very elements which make acceptable his turning to God and his praying because man's recognition of his own insignificance has a moral value in itself. On the other hand, God does shun the person who comes to Him with a sense of self-importance. As Rashi, the

---

[7]   Ibid., p. 184.

[8]   Cf. Berkovits, p. 75, and *Midrash Tehillim* (*Midrash on the Psalms*), Solomon Buber edition, chap. 55, section 6.

eleventh-century French-Jewish commentator *par excellence* of the Jewish Written and Oral Law, explains: "The higher a man's position, the more humble he must stand before God"[9] if he wishes to claim Divine attention. This was also Julie's remonstration to Saint-Preux, accusing him of an excessive sense of pride, of "philosophical haughtiness" that disdains the "simplicity of the Christian," and advising him: "Let us be humble,"[10] for we must preserve in ourselves the feeling of our weakness if we wish to address God. The Vicar, too, talked of his "insufficiency."[11]

The *Midrash* illustrates this idea by quoting from Isaiah lvii. 15 where we read:

> For thus saith the High and Lofty One
> That inhabiteth eternity, whose name is holy:
> I dwell in the high and holy place,
> With him also that is of a contrite and humble spirit.
> To revive the spirit of the humble,
> And to revive the heart of the contrite ones.

Paying close attention to these words of the prophet, the *Midrash* observes: "Even though He is the High and Lofty One, He dwells with the one of a contrite and humble spirit."[12] The contrasting positions of philosophy and religion with reference to prayer thus become vividly outlined. They talk "at cross purposes about prayer," notes Berkovits, "because they have divergent concepts about God."[13] To many philosophers, God is the High and Lofty One and one cannot pray to such a distant and impersonal God. According to Kant, who sees God as closer and more personal, one still should not "importune" Him with requests. To religion, however, the crucial aspect is that, though High and Lofty, God is also close and infinitely merciful and "bends down" so to speak—"comes down" is the term

---

[9] Berkovits, p. 76. See also Rashi (acronym of R̲abbi -S̲hlomo—Solomon—I̲tzhaki) of Troyes, France, in his clarification of Talmud, tractate of *Berakhoth*, p. 34b.

[10] Cf. *La Nouvelle Héloïse*, O.C. II, 672, and the present inquiry, Chapter VII, Section D.

[11] Cf. *La Profession de foi*, O.C. IV, 581: "Pénétré de mon insuffisance...."

[12] Cf. Berkovits, pp. 76–77, and *Midrash on Psalms*, chap. 4, section 3.

[13] Berkovits, p. 76.

used by the Bible[14]—to be near the humble and the contrite and to listen to their prayers, requests included. Those philosophers' God, on the other hand, and even Kant's God, is great but not great enough since He is either completely aloof from man as in deism or, in Kant's case, man ought not to beseech Him with his personal needs and requests. Such a God is High and Lofty but not near the humble and the contrite. However, God as seen by religion "bends down" and listens to prayer because His omnipotence is at one with His infinite mercy which makes it, as we said before, that He likes to be imposed upon, He likes to be approached by man, He is in search of the company of man, His highest creature. Prayer is really meaningful only on the basis of a view of God as closely involved with humble and insignificant man for whom He has infinite mercy, and that is theism. With this perspective in mind, noting that the Savoyard Vicar addressed his prayers to the "merciful and bounteous God,"[15] and Julie said: "The God that I serve is a merciful God, a Father: what moves me most is His goodness,"[16] we find that Jean-Jacques was closer to a theistic conception of Divinity than to a deistic one.

To the religionist, one cannot stress it too often, God is both transcendent and immanent. Both aspects are expressed in the religious literature of Judaism, including Isaiah and the *Midrash* that we have quoted, and are common-place in the Psalms. Thus when the psalmist, looking up to the sky, praised God in the words: "The heavens declare the glory of God, and the firmament showeth His handiwork," he was aware of Divine omnipotence and omniscience. Yet, he was able to conclude that very psalm with a prayer often repeated in Jewish liturgy: "May the words of my mouth and the meditation of my heart be pleasing to Thee, O Lord, my Rock and my Redeemer."[17] He could do so because he realized that with God's greatness goes also God's concern for and closeness to man. It is within this underlying belief in God's concern and closeness that prayer has a meaningful place. Reading Rousseau's prayers, it is obvious that they are addressed to a God whom he regards as concerned and close to him,

---

14   Exodus, xix.20 is just one example among many others.
15   Cf. *La Profession de foi*, O.C. IV, 592: "O être clément et bon."
16   *La Nouvelle Héloïse*, O.C. II, 696.
17   Psalm xix.

showing again that Rousseau's view of God is theistic rather than deistic.

Rousseau's theism is also apparent from the following considerations. Bible-based religion believes that God revealed Himself in both
nature and the Bible. Psalm xix to which we referred before is an excellent example of the two sources of knowledge of God available to
man: verses two to seven speak of God's revelation in nature as seen
in the starry heavens which "declare the glory of God," and verses
eight to twelve speak of the revelation of the Divine will in the Bible,
"the Torah (teaching) of the Lord is perfect, restoring the soul" (the
last verses, thirteen to fifteen, being a prayer for help from God who
is close, listening and reliable). Jean-Jacques had difficulty in accepting revelation in the Scriptures. He specifically referred to the Gospels
which he admired but where he encountered insoluble dilemmas.[18]
He remained, therefore, with revelation in nature alone where he
found goodness and mercy. The Vicar has thus said: "I adore the Supreme Power and am filled with tender emotions in view of the benefits which He confers. I need no one to teach me this religion; it is
dictated by nature herself."[19] To discover in nature some basic principles of natural religion, the Vicar tells us, he had to resort to reason.
He had arrived thus at the concept of a Supreme Intelligence in the
universe. Talking about that concept, he adds: "I attach to this name
[of God] the attributes of intelligence, power, will." These are related
and we can accept them as logically understandable. But Rousseau
continues and says: "and [I attach to God the attribute of] goodness
which is necessarily inferred from the preceding."[20] We do not quite
see how goodness necessarily follows from those other attributes. Our
feeling is that Jean-Jacques added it not as a logical consequence of
his reasoning but rather as a need of his heart for, as Pascal said, the
heart has reasons which reason does not know. And it is to this attribute of goodness that Rousseau's prayers will be addressed and
thereby will make sense, for God's goodness and mercy can be ap-

---

[18] Cf. *Profession de foi*, p. 627: "Avec tout cela ce même Evangile est plein de choses
incroyables...."

[19] Ibid., p. 583: "J'adore la puissance suprême et je m'attendris sur ses bienfaits. Je
n'ai pas besoin qu'on m'enseigne ce culte, il m'est dicté par la nature elle-même."

[20] Ibid., p. 581.

pealed to. But by doing so, Jean-Jacques asserts a theistic position, far from the deism of others.[21]

Furthermore, despite his claim that he resorts to reason in the formulation of his religious principles the Vicar, early in his discourse, states: "I also understood that, far from freeing me of my unnecessary doubts, the philosophers will only increase those that torment me and resolve none of the others. I, therefore, took another guide and said to myself: Let us consult the inner light, it will mislead me less than they would."[22] A new criterion, besides reason, is hereby introduced: the "inner light" which Grimsley defines as "the intuitive certainty of immediate consciousness."[23] With that inner light later also called by Rousseau "conscience, infallible judge of good and evil,"[24] we are moving away again from deism and its exclusive reliance on reason and entering back into the domain of theistic religion.

---

[21] We are aware that, in the context of trying to present all of God's qualities as rationally deductible, the Vicar defines God's goodness to suit this purpose in a very special, uncommon way as "love of order" (ibid., p. 593). A year later, in 1763, in his *Letter to M. de Beaumont*, Rousseau will quote from what the Vicar had said and repeat the definition of goodness as "love of order" (O.C. IV, 959) and, by doing so, show openly and directly that the Vicar's position is also his. However, when the Vicar addresses God in prayer as *clément et bon*, "merciful and good" (p. 592), it seems to us that the association of *bon* with *clément* implies the meaning of good (or bounteous, kind) in the generally accepted meaning of the term. The same is apparent when the Vicar says that "the nature of goodness…seems to me inseparable from the Divine essence" (p. 591). Earlier, in his writings, in his *Letter to Voltaire on Providence* (1756), Rousseau had asked: "Why should we desire to justify His omnipotence at the expense of His goodness?" (O.C. IV, 1061) in which goodness also appears in its usual meaning. It seems, therefore, that usually Rousseau employs *bon* in its common dictionary meaning and that it also has this meaning in the description of the qualities of God, notwithstanding its rationalistic definition by the Vicar in attempting to deduce God's qualities from nature and the repetition of that definition of God in his letter to M. de Beaumont. Rousseau has transposed the term goodness from revelation in religion to revelation in nature and redefined it as "love of nature" because one cannot speak of goodness in the sense of love of people in nature. Nonetheless, for all practical purposes when he addresses God, he reverts back to the usual, dictionary meaning of the term.

[22] Cf. *Profession de foi*, O.C. IV, 569.

[23] Cf. Grimsley, *Religious Writings*, p. 123, note 4.

[24] Cf. O.C. IV, 600–601.

Guyot concurs: "We are here moving away from Voltairian deism,"[25] while Guéhenno characterizes this "innermost feeling" as a "personal protest against the sophistry of reason."[26] To make God accessible, more than cold reason is indeed needed and Jean-Jacques felt it and expressed it in an essentially theistic posture. In the process, he also steered clear of Christian dogmas and his religion came to resemble more and more the universal Noahide religion at the dawn of mankind.

An attitude that should underlie petitionary prayer is offered by the modern scholar and theologian Dr. Joseph B. Soloveitchik whom we have referred to before. He stresses the fact that, as its Hebrew name *Tehinah* suggests, it is an unearned grace that we are requesting, something not due to us. It, therefore, must always be presented without any claim of worthiness or deserving and with full consciousness that we are asking for a special gift of God. In addition, though there be many emotions leading us to resort to prayer, the ones singled out as central for petitionary prayer are the feelings of our dependence and our helplessness. Rousseau's emphasis on humility coincides with this view. But for petitionary prayer, something more yet is required—an awareness of our dependence and helplessness to which God, in His mercy, responds.

As we have said at the beginning of this chapter, the admissibility of prayers of request is an issue in Rousseau's conception of prayer. This study would, therefore, be incomplete without a discussion of the problems specific to petitionary prayer, including the supposed purpose and efficacy of such prayer. If God has destined us to receive a given benefit, is not our asking for it superfluous? And if He has decided that we should not receive it, are we asking that He change His will? We shall present the answer to these questions as formulated in the writings of Joseph Albo, the Jewish classic authority in this field.[27]

Regarding the first question where the argument is that if God has determined to grant a benefit, there is no need for prayer, Albo explains that prayer is still useful, nay necessary. For God's decree is

---

[25] Cf. Guyot, p. 34: "Nous nous écartons ici du déisme voltairien."

[26] Cf. Guéhenno, II, 233.

[27] Joseph Albo, *Sefer Ha'ikkarim—Book of Principles*, trans. from the Hebrew by Isaac Husik (Philadelphia: Jewish Publication Society, 1930), Book 4, chap. 18.

always conditional. Only if man keeps on deserving the benefit by maintaining his good deeds and by right praying will the good decree be applied. But if not, it may be cancelled.

To the opposite question as to how prayer can avail if God has determined not to grant man the benefit he requests, Albo answers that, by praying, man can become a changed, better individual or, at least, manifest his intention to become such a good, deserving individual who may then deserve the requested benefit. For prayer, Albo reminds us, is not a mere recitation of words. Right praying is a deed which reflects the process of transformation that takes place within man. The man who turns his heart to God in prayer, in sincerity and truth, becomes, as a result of this act, of this deed, a different personality, not the same man spiritually that he was before he prayed. Then, the Divine decree may change to correspond to the new state of the worshiper. For basically, real praying leads to repentance, and repentance creates a new personality to which the former decree, by rights, no longer applies.[28]

---

[28] C.F. D'Arcy in the *Encyclopaedia of Religion and Ethics*, 1928, Vol. X, poses the problem from a different angle and resolves it with a reply similar to Albo's. He says that the moral or theological objection to prayers of petition is that making requests of God may be construed as a manifestation of doubt in God's omniscience. Hence, it is inferred that the only justifiable prayer is the prayer of resignation or submission to the will of God. In his answer, he states that since true prayer involves the bringing of the human will in harmony with the Divine will, it follows that to every change for the better, every upward movement of the human soul, there is a corresponding Divine response to the new capacity of the soul to receive greater Divine blessings. The error in the original argument was in its attributing to God a "mechanical rigidity" which is non-existent in Divine nature (p. 172).

To the scientific objection that everything in nature is a perfectly determined system, hence prayers for material benefits are impossible as we cannot ask of God to change His laws, D'Arcy replies that within the limits of natural laws there are many possible options which can be resorted to without violating natural law (pp. 172–73).

Among what D'Arcy calls "minor objections" is the argument of the "littleness of man." We recall that Saint-Preux has this in mind when he remonstrates that it is improper for God to take care of each individual. The reply of D'Arcy is first that man is also a spiritual being, therefore a creature of importance to God, and secondly that God's greatness and perfection demand that He consider everyone as having significance in His sight (p. 174). We presented a similar argument before, that God's greatness resides precisely in His relating to the humble

The same principle is utilized by Albo to answer the general theological question formulated by philosophers as follows: if God's will is unchangeable, how can prayer or anything else change it? Again, the answer is that while God's will is unchangeable, His decrees are not. Indeed, it is God's will that each man's fate should *not* be immutable but should depend on his deeds and his merit. That is why a change to the better in a man's worthiness, partly brought about by prayer but mainly reflected by it, can, indeed, bring about a change in the decree facing him. As Albo puts it: "The Divine will in the first place is that the decree should be realized *if*[29] the person in question continues in the same state, and that the decree should be changed if the person's state changes."[30]

Obviously, Albo's formulation is accepted as authoritative in Judaism because it summarizes well Jewish tradition. As the *Midrash* states: "Prayer is only heard if a person makes his heart soft…through return (repentance) to God."[31] Prayer in Judaism as in Rousseau[32] is defined as "service of the heart,"[33] and "the change of the hardened heart is the essence of right praying."[34]

Thus, God's will as understood by Judaism is that every decree should be conditional upon man's behavior, subject to change if the person changes. And prayer is one crucial instrument for human change to be better. This conditionality of God's decrees, central to Jewish and probably to Christian thought, seems to have been either totally overlooked or rejected by the Vicar (i.e. Rousseau) who followed Malebranche's ideas in this respect. Like many other philosophers, Malebranche regarded God's decrees as absolute and unrelated to an individual's future behavior and his and the Vicar's criticism of petitionary prayer stem from this central assumption which, as a corollary, also rules out personal providence, reward and

---

and contrite and that man's insignificance and insufficiency are elements pleasing to God who shuns those who display their self-importance. We have also stressed that God likes to be imposed on.

[29] The italics are ours.

[30] Cf. Albo, Vol IV, chap. 18, p. 165. Quoted in Berkovits, p. 79.

[31] Cf. *Midrash on Psalms*, chap. 65, section 2. Quoted in Berkovits, p. 79.

[32] Cf. O.C.IV, 627: The Vicar says: "Le culte essentiel est celui du coeur."

[33] Cf. Talmud, tractate of *Taanith*, p. 2a.

[34] Cf. Berkovits, p. 79.

punishment and perhaps even mercy, leaving everything to remote autocratic arbitrariness.

Prayer in the *Correspondance* of Rousseau

A. *Letter to M. De Franquières* (1769)

1. Prayer of Trust in God's Judgment

Jean-Jacques had become, most probably despite himself, a spiritual guide and counselor. Those who turned to him with religious problems were both clergymen and laymen who felt that he would understand them best because he, too, had not only written about but had also struggled with religious issues and yet emerged as the religious man he considered himself to be. Moreover, he had breadth of understanding and tolerance coupled with an attitude, ability and desire to preserve and, if possible, to enhance the self-esteem of the inquirer.

Nothing is known about M. de Franquières except that he probably was a nobleman from the Dauphiné, that he had religious doubts and that he turned to Jean-Jacques for guidance in two letters. Rousseau tried to clarify the problems raised and offer solutions as well as bring some peace of mind to his correspondent. His long answer, dated January 15, 1769, was written in a relaxed style and gives us the last systematic and coherent presentation of his religious views.

The problem of the existence of evil in the world has baffled people in all climes and ages. The eighteenth century, too, has had its share of calamities, among which was the tragic disaster of the earthquake in Lisbon. In his letter to M. de Franquières, Jean-Jacques also speaks of moral evil which he attributes not to God but to man's crimes and man's abuse of his freedom of will. Only few are those who have not abused their free will and Rousseau admires them, for they are a credit and an honor to humanity. He, too, in a short prayer, tells us that he wishes to be counted among them:

> "My God! Give me virtues and place me some day close to the Fénelons, Catons, Socrates! What will the rest of mankind matter to me? I will not blush for having been a man."[1]

Only seven years separate this letter from *Emile* where the Vicar (like Saint-Preux before him) feels that God had already given him reason so that he may know what is good, conscience so that he may love it and liberty in order that he may choose it.[2] Prayers of petition were then at best tolerated but not resorted to oneself. Yet, here, Rousseau does exactly that. He wants God to give him the strength to do good."Give me virtues," he says, this time talking himself and not through a fictitious spokesman. When relaxed and at ease, as is the case during the writing of this letter, Jean-Jacques does not go into subtleties of opposition to such prayers but only affirms what he deeply feels to be true. To his spokesmen, Saint-Preux and the Vicar, however, he assigned the role of philosophically contending over this issue.

Rousseau singles out three personalities who are highly esteemed by him and who, he believes, must occupy a special place of honor in the world beyond, for they have justified and redeemed mankind in the sight of God. Rousseau's prayer is that he be found worthy of taking his place near them. The three are: Fénelon, French theologian and writer, Cato, Roman statesman, soldier and writer, and Socrates, the Athenian philosopher. From the writings of Rousseau, let us present just a few reasons as to what may have attached him to these three in particular. What was their kinship of ideas?

---

[1] Cf. *Correspondance*, 1933, Vol. XIX, letter 3781, p. 57 and cf. O.C. IV, 1141–42: "Mon Dieu! donne-moi des vertus, et me place un jour auprès des Fénelon, des Caton, des Socrate. Que m'importera le reste du genre humain? Je ne rougirai point d'avoir été homme."

[2] *La Nouvelle Héloïse*, Part 6, letter 7, O.C. II, 683. See also *Profession de foi*, O.C. IV, 605.

Fénelon: Rousseau loved nature and admired many passages in *Télémaque* in which the author evoked nature as a framework and did so in flattering our sight by his description in most cheerful colors.[3] Moreover, the goodness of human nature and not its corruption was stressed by Fénelon, something which Jean-Jacques also believed in and in which he was glad to receive some backing by an official representative of the Church. Both utilized this concept as their basis for a system of education which develops and does not counteract nature. The Vicar's first argument on the existence of God as the Unmoved Mover goes back to Aristotle but was recently used by Fénelon in his *Traité de l'existence de Dieu*.[4] Related to this concept is the denial by both about creation being the result of *quantité des jets*, for God does not play dice and the world, therefore, is not the result of accident. In his letter to a doubter, the abbé de Carondelet from Paris, Jean-Jacques reveals his high regard for Fénelon's integrity by telling the abbé that anyone having scruples which Fénelon did not have would become suspect in his, Rousseau's, eyes.[5] We also have Rousseau's assertion that affectionate and gentle souls do not believe in hell, and this led him to be astonished to see good Fénelon speak of it in his *Télémaque* as if he really believed in it. Here, however, Jean-Jacques humorously suggests that a bishop has to tell a lie sometimes,[6] thereby exculpating the prelate he admired from holding such a view. Both also shared many other traits which make for affinity: both were individualists, complex, political reformers, possessed original ideas and were prosecuted and persecuted for their religious ideas (quiétisme for Fénelon).

Cato: Jean-Jacques quotes approvingly what Cicero made Cato say: "I do not regret having lived since I have lived in such a way that I deem that I was not born in vain.[7] Rousseau also felt he had taught humanity and served it well. In his long monologue, the Vicar asked: "Why would I wish to be like Cato who tears his entrails rather than

---

[3] Van Tieghem, p. 125.
[4] Cf. *Profession de foi*, O.C. IV, 576 and Grimsley, *Religious Writings*, p. 132, note 1.
[5] Cf. *Correspondance*, 1928, Vol. X, letter 2000, p. 290.
[6] Cf. Masson, *La Profession de foi de Rousseau*, p. 221.
[7] Cf. *Lettre à Voltaire sur la Providence*, O.C. IV, 1064.

triumphant Caesar?"[8] Masson states that the formula "who tears his entrails" is dear to Rousseau when he speaks of the suicide of Cato. From all the heroes celebrated by Plutarch, the "great and Divine Cato" is the one to whom Rousseau devotes a lifelong, faithful admiration.[9] In his chapter on Civil Religion, Jean-Jacques also takes notice of the fact that Cato refuted Caesar who had maintained that the soul was mortal.[10] We know how strong was Rousseau's belief in the immortality of the soul which alone provides him with an acceptable answer to the problem of the suffering of the just.

Socrates: Socrates had long been regarded as the most eminent of the "saints of paganism."[11] Some, like Father Lamy whom Rousseau held in high esteem, frequently referred to Socrates as one of the thinkers who, sometimes unknown to himself, was working for the glory of God and the Christian Church.[12] Rousseau was among the first, Grimsley notes, to establish a close parallel between Socrates and Jesus.[13] The Vicar will say: "If the life and death of Socrates are of a sage, the life and death of Jesus are of a God."[14] Though this statement does not imply any acceptance of the divinity of Jesus or his incarnation—fundamental to Christianity—it was meant to be complimentary to Jesus whose disciple Rousseau claimed to be[15] and to Socrates whom he recognized as a sage for his emancipatory work. In his letter to M. de Franquières, Jean-Jacques notes that, without hope for an after-life, Socrates would have been at pains to act well in this world.[16] This, of course, forms a strong link between Socrates and Rousseau who constantly emphasizes life after death. Jean-Jacques will also draw a parallel between what he calls "the Hebrew sage and the Greek sage" and call himself "an admirer of one and of the other."[17]

[8] Ibid., *Profession de foi*, p. 596.
[9] Cf. Masson, *La Profession de foi de Rousseau*, p. 245.
[10] Cf. *Du contrat social* (Religion civile), O.C. III, 468.
[11] Cf. Masson, *La Profession de foi de Rousseau*, p. 407.
[12] Cf. Grimsley, *Religious Writings*, p. 12.
[13] Ibid., p. 189, note 4.
[14] Cf. *Profession de foi*, p. 626.
[15] Cf. *Lettre à M. de Beaumont*, O.C. IV, 960.
[16] Ibid., p. 1144.
[17] Ibid., p. 1145.

Each of these three heroes, Fénelon, Cato and Socrates, exemplifies those great men who have not misused their freedom of will but have used it in such a way that, according to Rousseau, they may be held to be assets to humanity. Jean-Jacques who is painfully aware that he has been misunderstood by his contemporaries can now afford to say that the "rest of mankind" will not matter to him. For he will not have any reason to "blush for having been a man" when vindicated by God in placing him next to those who, in his opinion, have achieved eternal life. That it be so is his ardent prayer.

2. Prayer to God as Divine Witness

Elaborating on the sufferings of the righteous, Jean-Jacques finds consolation in the hope of an after-life, beyond death, and in the belief—fundamental to him—that man is acting under the watchful and scrutinizing eye of God who is the ever-present Divine witness. This again sets him apart from the *philosophes* and the deists who do not accept personal providence, the "scrutinizing eye of God," following each individual human being. To Rousseau, the awareness of such a presence leads to an expression of satisfaction that there is the Divine Somebody who knows the truth. He then offers a brief prayer and voices his delight at the thought of being able to render a good account of himself before God:

> "It is always pleasant in adversity to have someone to witness that you did not deserve it; there is a feeling of pride truly worthy of virtue in being able to say to God: 'Thou who canst read in my heart, Thou seest that it is as a just man and staunch of soul that I use the freedom which Thou hast granted me'"[18]

This short prayer contains an affirmation of man's freedom of will, as opposed to a more deterministic viewpoint by Voltaire for instance. It also breathes with confidence because Jean-Jacques who feels so misunderstood by society, including the *philosophes*, finds comfort and strength in the idea that God who rights all wrongs, if

---

[18] Cf. *Correspondance*, XIX, 60, and *O.C.* IV 1144: "C'est toujours une douceur dans l'adversité d'avoir un témoin qu'on ne l'a pas méritée; c'est un orgueil vraiment digne de la vertu de pouvoir dire à Dieu: 'Toi qui lis dans mon coeur, tu vois que j'use en âme forte et en homme juste de la liberté que tu m'as donnée.'"

not in this world, then in the next, sees deep in his heart and knows that his intentions, if not always his deeds, were good and meant to please the Creator. The quality of justice which in Rousseau's outlook is predominant with regard to God's attribute of justice is equally fundamental in regard to man. Some eight years hence, Rousseau will hand out in Paris a self-defending circular of his addressed to "Every Frenchman who still loves justice and truth."

Throughout his writings, Rousseau concretizes the Divine presence by the metaphor of the eternal eye, ever looking at man. Observes Masson: "The soul of Rousseau has a need to be religious...for the full blooming of all its powers. It would suffocate in a world without God. He needs God in order to exist."[19] Being the object of God's gaze gives meaning to his life. It tells him that what he does has importance since God takes notice of it. That gaze, however, can also be uncomfortable if one feels that he has fallen short of the high goals and high expectations he has set for himself. But that is not the case of Jean-Jacques. He is relaxed and at peace with himself and apparently with God when he writes these lines, for he feels that God who has been witness to his life sees him as he sees himself "a just man and staunch of soul." Full of optimism, he, therefore, adds after his prayer and thinking about himself: "The true believer who everywhere believes himself to be watched over by the eternal eye delights in boasting before Heaven that he has fulfilled his duties upon this earth."[20]

This metaphor of the eternal seeing eye also has most important implications for the overall theme of the present study—prayer in the writings of Rousseau. For if God is always present, always looking at man, then relating to Divinity becomes an urgent matter for man wherever he may be and not only in the limited physical precincts of a house of worship. All of life is then lived under the gaze of God and, therefore, life assumes a new vertical dimension. Relating to and communicating with the Divine eye that looks at us becomes a neces-

---

[19] Cf. Masson, *La Religion de Rousseau*, II, 258: "L'âme de Rousseau a besoin d'être religieuse...pour le plein épanouissement de toutes ses puissances. Elle étoufferait dans un univers sans Dieu. Dieu lui est nécessaire pour exister."

[20] Cf. *Correspondance*, XIX, 60, and *O.C.* IV, 1144: "Le vrai croyant, qui se sent partout sous l'oeil éternel, aime à s'honorer à la face du ciel d'avoir rempli ses devoirs sur la terre."

sity and prayer becomes of paramount value. Writing on the perspective of the Divine seeing eye, Burgelin contrasts deism with Rousseau's philosophy which we call theism. He says: "Deism does not raise the philosopher beyond [a concept of God as] the Great Mechanic whom our affairs do not concern. Rousseau does not accept this deaf God. Prayer is the important act in which we heighten our awareness of the Divine presence."[21] Furthermore, the belief in Divine existence enables man to feel in his heart, says Jean-Jacques, that he has a "confidant to his thoughts."[22] In these terms, Rousseau describes what must be a close relationship with a God who is in one's proximity (and not the remote God of deism). Interestingly, Dr. Berkovits in his essay on prayer uses the very same expression to characterize the man-God relationship. He writes: "To pray means to make God *the confidant* of one's sorrow and need. The asking and begging are natural enough, but they are of *secondary importance*."[23] In our prayer, Jean-Jacques, the lonely man and *promeneur*, derives comfort and encouragement from this concept of being ever in presence of the watchful eye of Divinity while, to protect himself from some hostile contemporaries, he had to seek anonymity by signing this letter with a borrowed penname "Renou."

B. Letter to Monsieur Moultou (1769)

Prayer about the After-Life

Rousseau's Letter to M. de Franquières was written, as we have seen, on January 15, 1769, in Bourgoin. Almost one month later, on February 14, 1769, this time from Monquin to which he had moved, Jean-Jacques wrote another letter on a similar theme of offering guidance to people who have religious doubts. This letter is addressed to Monsieur Moultou and was forwarded to Montpellier. From other letters, we find that his full name was Paul-Claude Moultou and that he was a minister of the Holy Gospel ("ministre du

---

[21] Cf. Burgelin, *La Philosophie de l'existence*, p. 460.
[22] Cf. *O.C.* IV, 1144: "confident de ses pensées."
[23] Cf. Berkovits, p. 28. The italcis are ours.

St. Evangile") in Geneva. It bears the number 3795 and is printed in the *General Correspondence of J.-J. Rousseau.*[24]

Jean-Jacques thinks the end of his life is not far and looks forward—with joy, he says—to his sojourn in the world beyond, following the injustice and the misfortunes he has suffered in this world. Awaiting that event, his only preoccupation is to leave this world with the same innocence with which he has lived.

The core of this letter deals with Rousseau's response to the religious doubts of Paul Moultou. Again, a number of ideas and arguments dear to him, some of which appeared in his letter to M. de Franquières, are repeated here. First and above all is the assertion that man shall be judged ("on sera jugé"). In other words, there exists a Divine Judge who will ask for accounts and, therefore, man must act responsibly. Related to it is the oft-repeated conviction of Jean-Jacques that man will be judged on his deeds which depend on him and not on his beliefs (for "sincere unbelief is not a crime"). Rousseau also makes a distinction between a person who has never believed whom he is willing to condone and a person who has believed before and now claims not to believe—such seems to be the case of Moultou—and this Rousseau cannot excuse, countenance or accept. Cessation of belief is not understandable to Rousseau. For to him, belief is the natural inclination of man and doubt can be only temporary. He who once believed cannot, therefore, stop believing. Jean-Jacques consequently insists that his correspondent honestly examine his heart to determine whether he really is in good faith with himself. Then, Rousseau enumerates basic proofs for the existence of God, such as universal intelligence, moral instinct, inner voice, plus the implication that disbelief leads to materialism and removes morality from human life—and that, we know, is crucial to Rousseau. It is at this point that he invokes God in a quasi-prayer, with God being more a witness to Rousseau's interjections than being directly addressed. Here, too, for the first time in a prayer does he make reference to Jesus though not in any Divine sense:

> O God! can it be that a just and ill-fated man who has been subjected to all the ills of this life and has not even been spared humiliation and disgrace,

---

[24] Cf. *Correspondance*, XIX 87–90.

has no hope of compensation in the after-life, and has to die like a beast, having lived like a God? No, no, Moultou. Jesus, whom this century has failed to appreciate because it was unworthy of understanding him, who died because he tried to change his base compatriots into an illustrious and virtuous people, that sublime Jesus, did not die completely on the cross: and I am but a weak and wretched man, yet one who is conscious of never having allowed his heart to be sullied by any guilty feeling, and this is enough to make the awareness of my approaching dissolution be accompanied by certainty about the after-life. The whole of nature assures me of this. Nature is not self-contradictory. I discern in it an admirable physical order which is never at variance with itself. The moral order must correspond to this physical order. Yet in my case it was upset during my whole life: it will therefore come into force with my death.[25]

After having given general proofs for the existence of God, Jean-Jacques becomes more personal in this prayer. For what he says has particular relevance to his own life and is consequently verbalized in emotional tones: the sufferings of the just man, of the righteous man, in this world cry out for the existence of an after-life in which justice will be meted out and accounts redressed. It is impossible for the just man, Rousseau insists, "to die like a beast," to have a common fate with the beast. We are reminded here of Ecclesiastes who said in a mood of darkest pessimism: "For that which befalleth the sons of men befalleth beasts;...as the one dieth, so dieth the other...so that man hath no pre-eminence above a beast, for all is vanity."[26] Would an identical fate be shared by man and beast? Is there really no advan-

---

[25]   Cf. English translation in Guéhenno, II, 234, and original French in *Correspondance*, XIX, 88–89: "Eh quoi, mon Dieu! le juste infortuné en proie à tous les maux de cette vie, sans en excepter même l'opprobre et le déshonneur, n'aurait nul dédommagement à attendre après elle, et mourrait en bête après avoir vécu en Dieu? Non, non, Moultou; Jésus que ce siècle a méconnu, parce qu'il est indigne de le connaître; Jesus, qui mourut pour avoir voulu faire un peuple illustre et vertueux de ses vils compatriotes, le sublime Jésus ne mourut point tout entier sur la croix; et moi qui ne suis qu'un chétif homme plein de faiblesses, mais qui me sens un coeur dont un sentiment coupable n'approcha jamais, c'en est assez pour qu'en sentant approcher la dissolution de mon corps je sente en même temps la certitude de vivre. La nature entière m'en est garante. Elle n'est pas contradictoire avec elle-même: j'y vois régner un ordre physique admirable et qui ne se dément jamais. L'ordre moral y doit correspondre. Il fut pourtant renversé pour moi durant toute ma vie; il va donc commencer à ma mort."

[26]   Ecclesiastes, iii.19.

tage of man over the beast? This is intolerable, unacceptable, to Rousseau and he tells it to us in his double "no" to Moultou. Then, suddenly he resorts to bringing up the case of Jesus. Guéhenno provides us with one possible reason: "Nietzsche, in moods of exaltation, turned to Dionysos, so Jean-Jacques turned to Jesus."[27] Perhaps it is so. We feel, however, that the example of Jesus imposes itself to him because what he adds about Jesus is applicable to him, Rousseau, too, and so he identifies with Jesus. Thus, when Jean-Jacques says: "Jesus whom this century has failed to appreciate because it was unworthy of understanding him," he thinks about his own situation, being unappreciated by his contemporaries, and about his own moral superiority or at the very least, his innocence. The motivation of the rejection is also analogous: "because he tried to change his base compatriots into an illustrious and virtuous people." Is not this what Jean-Jacques, too, had tried to do? For Rousseau, let us not forget, has always considered himself as a teacher and a benefactor of humanity. The ending up with the belief that Jesus "did not die completely on the cross" suggests that he, Rousseau, will not die completely either after a life of suffering. That he deserves immortality is taken for granted. For though he qualifies himself as "a weak and wretched man," he is firm in pleading innocence (his heart was never "sullied by any guilty feelings") and that gives him not only assurance but certainty of life after death.

Following this mainly moral necessity of immortality to compensate for sufferings in this world, Rousseau adds the argument of the orderliness of nature which suggests a corresponding moral orderliness in the universe, and since that order was upset in his life, it must come after his death.

Rousseau says in this prayer that the eighteenth century did fail to appreciate Jesus, something for which he blames his "unworthy" contemporaries. However, when talking about Jesus trying to change his own contemporaries, Rousseau blames the lack of success on the "base" compatriots of Jesus. We take exception to the adjective "base" ("vils" compatriotes).

In general, Jean-Jacques refers to the Jewish people with sympathy and understanding. He can identify with their being persecuted

---

[27]   Cf. Guéhenno, II 234.

unjustly throughout the centuries. He speaks of them as being tyran-nized and dealt with cruelly. He says that only poverty-stricken, ig-norant or mercenary Jews could be induced to convert or to speak out against Judaism, but their sages would only smile silently at such in-ducements.[28] He has noticed their circumspectness and their reluc-tance in talking with him and about Judaism and understands well the reason thereof. For "the unfortunate people feel that they are in our arbitrary power; the tyranny that is exerted toward them renders them apprehensive."[29] He realizes that Jews could speak their mind fully and truly only if the situation of the Jewish people were normal-ized by the creation of "a free State, with schools and universities of their own wherein they could speak and debate without any risk"[30] which, in capsule form, is the rationale that led to the establishment of the State of Israel close to two hundred years later. Finally, in a gener-alization about "the three main religions in Europe," he says: "The re-ligion which admits only one revelation is the oldest and, it would seem, the surest [to be correct? dependable?]."[31] Masson also saw in these passages "the secret sympathy toward Judaism which one can guess in Rousseau"[32] and he supports his finding by a quote from Le Franc de Pompignan who wrote that "with regard to the Jews, the Citizen of Geneva seems to have, one does not know why, a singular predilection for their religion."[33] In addition, Masson calls our atten-tion to some unpublished writings of Rousseau which he found in Rousseau's notebooks ("cahiers de brouillons") where there are two pages of comments on the vitality of the Jewish people which end as follows: "Any man, whoever he might be, must recognize in them a unique wonder, the Divine or human causes of which certainly merit study and admiration by scholars, in preference to all that Greece and Rome offer us that is admirable in the line of political institutions and

---

[28] Cf. *Profession de foi du vicaire savoyard*, O.C. IV, 621.

[29] Ibid., p. 621.

[30] Ibid., p. 621. See also above Chapter III, Section B.

[31] Ibid., p. 619: "Celle qui n'admet qu'une révélation est la plus ancienne, et paraît la plus sûre."

[32] Cf. Masson, *La Profession de foi de J.-J. Rousseau*, p. 375, note 1: "la sympathie se-crète qui se laisse deviner chez Rousseau pour le judaïsme."

[33] Ibid., p. 375, note 1: "A l'égard des Juifs, le Citoyen de Genève paraît, on ne sait pourquoi, avoir une prédilection singulière pour leur religion."

human establishments."[34] In the light of these quotes and statements, it is incongruous to see Rousseau calling the ancient Judeans "base compatriots." How can one explain it? Possibly this way: when he expresses his own thoughts based on his own contact with Jews and what he knows of Judaism, he tends to a positive attitude toward them. However, when speaking of Jesus and the first century of our era, he follows the evaluation of Christian religious writings describing that period. This is especially so, since he probably sees a strong parallel between Jesus and himself, being so often attacked by his own "vile compatriots."

---

[34] Ibid., p. 375, note 1: 'Tout homme, quel qu'il soit, y doit reconnaître une merveille unique, dont les causes divines ou humaines méritent certainement l'étude et l'admiration des sages, préférablement à tout ce que la Grèce et Rome nous offrent d'admirable en fait d'institutions politiques et d'établissements humains. "This quatation as well as the full text of the two pages on the Jews in Rousseau's notebooks can be found in O.C. III 498–500, under the general division called "Fragments politiques"—with the specific reference number 24 in brackets [Des Juifs]. The original transcription was made by Miss Claire Rosselet former director or" the "Bibliothèque publique" de la ville de Neuchâtel, Suisse.

CHAPTER XI

Prayer in the *Confessions* (1765–1770)[1]

Prayer to the Supreme God

There is concensus of opinion among critics that by 1760 Rousseau had decided to write his autobiography and, for that purpose, began collecting documents and general material. A formal request to this effect was addressed to Jean-Jacques in a letter dated December 31, 1761 by his Genevan publisher from Holland, Marc-Michel Rey, who says: "One thing I have been ambitious of for a long time…is to have the history of your life." The wording "for a long time" indicates a prior demand. Rey wanted it as a preface to the collected works of Rousseau. At that time, the end of 1761, when he endured great physical discomfort, Rousseau also underwent a crisis. He convinced himself that the Jesuits were plotting to issue his forthcoming book *Emile* (1762) after his death in an altered form and add to it their own profession of faith. This caused his self-justification in four letters to Malesherbes in January 1762. Another crisis soon appeared in the offing: an anonymous libel published against him by Voltaire on January 1, 1765 and entitled *Sentiment of Citizens* ("Sentiment des citoyens"). The calumny was outright false only in part. Much of its impact was due to its revealing to the world the true fact of abandonment of his own children by the author of *Emile*.

Rousseau wrote the first six books of the *Confessions* from March 1765, soon after the above mentioned crisis, to August 1767 and the other six books in 1769 and 1770. He felt that in his *Confessions* he would tell everything and thus find exculpation. The original intent,

---

[1]   Written between 1765 and 1770 and published posthumously in 1782 (six books) and in 1789 (complete edition).

though, was to describe the history of a soul, but, in actuality, reacting to accusations, the *Confessions* became a work of self-defense, apologia and self-justification. Its sincerity strikes everyone who reads it and is beyond questioning. Its accuracy, however, is another matter. Involuntarily, lapses of memory occurred. Yet, in the opinion of George Havens: "Whatever the reader's final judgment may be about Rousseau, whether we are inclined to condemn or excuse [him], we need to remind ourselves that he has confessed not only his committed faults or sins but at times even the secret thoughts of which he later repented. It is a most exacting standard. Who, even of the best, would be prepared to meet it?"[2]

The opening of the *Confessions* immediately announces to the reader that this will be a special type of book, "without precedent." For in it the writer who considers himself different from all men will reveal himself as he is. Then, it states that on Judgment Day, the writer will not hesitate to appear before the sovereign Judge holding his book of *Confessions* in his hand and boldly state the following declaration to God ending in prayer:

> This is what I have done, what I have thought, what I was. I have told the good and the bad with equal frankness. I have neither omitted anything bad, nor interpolated anything good. If I have occasionally made use of some immaterial embellishments, this has only been in order to fill a gap caused by a lapse of my memory. I may have assumed the truth of that which I knew might have been true, never of that which I knew to be false. I have shown myself as I was: mean and contemptible, good, high-minded and sublime, according as I was one or the other. I have unveiled my inmost self even as Thou hast seen it. O Eternal Being! Gather around me the countless host of my fellow-men; let them hear my confessions, lament for my unworthiness, and blush for my imperfections. Then let each of them in turn reveal, with the same sincerity, the secrets of his heart at the foot of Thy throne and say, if he dare, "*I was better than that man!*"[3]

---

[2] Cf. George R. Havens, p. 283.

[3] *Les Confessions*, Book 1, O.C. I, 5: "Voilà ce que j'ai fait, ce que j'ai pensé, ce que je fus. J'ai dit le bien et le mal avec la même franchise. Je n'ai rien tu de mauvais, rien ajouté de bon, et s'il m'est arrivé d'employer quelque ornement indifférent, cela n'a jamais été que pour remplir un vide occasionné par mon défaut de mémoire; j'ai pu supposer vrai ce que je savais avoir pu l'être, jamais ce que je savais être faux. Je me suis montré tel que je fus, méprisable et vil quand je l'ai été,

This passage, placed at the beginning of the *Confessions*, introduces us immediately in a solemn tone to the apocalyptic vision of the author's projected appearance before the Supreme Judge to whom he confidently presents the written record of his life, expecting exoneration. In reality, while addressing God who is both witness and judge, Jean-Jacques is equally anxious of receiving human approval—something he did not receive too often during his turbulent life. He starts by asking the reader to suspend his judgment till he will have heard the case. But soon enough, Rousseau overwhelms us by his own verdict of innocence or "not guilty" of any willful offense, pronounced in presence of the Heavenly Court. He does no less than requesting of God to whom he talks as to a very familiar personality—perhaps an overcompensation, showing he is special to God if not to man, rather than a presumptuousness—and whom he asks in the imperative mode to "gather" all his fellow-men for some kind of public contest. This imperative "gather," Professor Lester G. Crocker notes, is followed by five exhortations: "let them hear…lament…blush…reveal…and say." All that leads up to a crescendo which no one will dare contradict, namely that "I was better than that man"—a stroke which "contains implicitly the desired judgment and wins assent of the reader-judge."[4] Prayer here is then used as a means of proclaiming one's own innocence in the context of addressing God.

Some have spoken of arrogance and audacity in this preamble to Rousseau's *Confessions* and have done so not without some reason or justification. Yet, .judged from a wider perspective, we find that what Jean-Jacques tries to convey to the reader is rather his singularity, his finding himself so different from other people, one of a kind, which makes him suffer more keenly than others—a state of being which neither gives him any privileges nor makes him worthier than others. It certainly adds no happiness to him. Just the contrary.

---

bon, généreux, sublime, quand je l'ai été: j'ai dévoilé mon intérieur tel que tu l'as vu toi-même. Etre éternel, rassemble autour de moi l'innombrable foule de mes semblables: qu'ils écoutent mes confessions, qu'ils gémissent de mes indignités, qu'ils rougissent de mes misères. Que chacun d'eux découvre à son tour son coeur aux pieds de ton trône avec la même sincérité; et puis qu'un seul te dise, s'il l'ose: *je fus meilleur que cet homme-là.*"

[4]   Lester G. Crocker, "Confessions de J.-J. Rousseau," *Explication de texte*, ed. Jean Sareil, Vol. I, 2nd ed. (Englewood Cliffs, N.J.: Prentice-Hall, 1970), pp. 161–62.

The statement that none would "dare" say to God that he was better than Jean-Jacques appears at first sight very striking and implying a certain self-righteousness and moral superiority. In fact, however, when looked at more closely, it reveals a man painfully aware of his own shortcomings despite his bravura, conditioned probably by wounded pride. That same awareness of shortcomings is also present in the 1764 *Letters Written from the Mountain*. In the first letter, anticipating the prelude to the *Confessions*, he thus declares that "full of confidence [I] hope one day to say to the Supreme Arbiter" the following prayer:

> "Deign judge in Thy clemency a weak man; I have done evil on earth but I have published this writing."[5]

This deep need for self-justification either at the Heavenly Court, as in the *Confessions* and in this first letter from the mountain, or at the human court, as evidenced by the end of his long *Letter to M. de Beaumont*,[6] is always accompanied by his self-defense in the form of a book containing his record, as he sees it, and spelling out the merit of his case. Need we add that he does not doubt the outcome of such a trial by a truly impartial court?

An intense desire to be completely sincere has ever been the goal and hallmark of Jean-Jacques, endearing him especially to young, idealistic readers. In this preamble to the *Confessions* his challenge to others is based on their showing "the same sincerity" that he has shown in revealing the secrets of his heart to God and to man.

Lest we be carried away by the moving sweep of Rousseau's confessions, Masson cautions us not to mistake Rousseau's thought, for he does not present himself as a hero or a saint but rather as the personification of the natural man: "He means to say that in no soul did nature show itself more natural, more loving of the good, more enamored of simplicity, of uprightness, of purity. If ever the secret of

---

5   Cf. *Lettres écrites de la montagne*, O.C. III, 697: "...moi qui, plein de confiance, espère un jour dire au Juge Suprême: daigne juger dans ta clémence un homme faible; j'ai fait le mal sur la terre, mais j'ai publié cet écrit."

6   Ibid., IV, 1007: "Monseigneur...Si vous étiez un particulier comme moi, que je puisse vous citer devant un tribunal équitable et que nous y comparussions tous deux, moi avec mon livre et vous avec votre mandement...."

nature were lost, it is in him that one would find it again…[for] it [nature] is [expressed] eminently in some selected souls or, another way of putting it, it is those souls that constitute living nature."[7]

We have noted here again that Jean-Jacques makes his appeal directly to the Sovereign Judge, with no need felt for an intermediary despite the knowledge of his shortcomings. In our prayer, too, is implied that one appears before the Heavenly Tribunal with the book of one's life in one's hands. In other words, man is judged by the record of his deeds and not by his beliefs. Furthermore, while his last prayers become more emotional, personal and petitionary, bringing them more in line with accepted modes of prayer in religions that believe in revelation and a personal God interested and responsive to individual human beings, Jean-Jacques did not redevelop a need to appeal to an intermediary to help atone for his acknowledged shortcomings by a special act of grace or intervention of God.

We have spoken here about the beginning of the *Confessions*. Toward the end of it, in book twelve, we find his conception of prayer as silent wonder which we have analyzed above.[8] Also included in the *Confessions* is a passage[9] revealing the extent to which natural beauty evoked in Rousseau religious feeling and a sense of communion with Divinity.

---

[7]   Cf. Masson, *La Religion de Rousseau*, II, 291–92.

[8]   Cf. *O.C.* I, Book 12, p. 642, and above Chapter VI, Section D.

[9]   Cf. ibid., Book 6, p. 236, and above Chapter V.

CHAPTER XII

Prayer in Rousseau Juge de Jean-Jacques
Dialogues (1772–1776)[1]

A. Proximity of Nature to God—Hymn to Solitude

This book of dialogues stands apart in Rousseau as little read and studied and almost without effect on literature. It reflects Rousseau's obsession with the idea of a universal plot against him. He was suspicious of a League that supposedly was formed against him and was headed by Choiseul in order to bring him dishonor. Though no such plot existed in fact, the fear of persecution did have some basis in reality. Robert Osmont observes: "The hostility toward him by the powerful of the time weighs on his relationships with other people."[2] There were also private undertakings against him by Voltaire and he had reason to worry about Mme du Deffand, Grimm and others.

Rousseau's presence in Paris in 1770 was irregular and fraught with danger for his safety and freedom of movement since the 1762 decree ("prise de corps") against him had not been repealed. Still, he returned to Paris to wage his fight. As no plot makes its appearance, he examines his situation around 1772, date of the first dialogue, and imagines a hypothesis of a plot. Problems of self-knowledge are debated at length in his second dialogue which occupied him during 1773 and part of 1774. Then, he calculates the chances of survival of his thought and of his message in the third dialogue written in 1774

---

[1]   Written between 1772 and 1776 and published posthumously by Brooke-Boothby in 1780 (first dialogue only) and by Mme de Sainte-Foy, niece of Condillac, on December 31, 1800 (all three dialogues).

[2]   Cf. *O.C.* I, Introduction by Robert Osmont, p. liv.

and 1775. The preface, entitled "On the Subject and the Form of this Writing" dates from the end of 1775. Finally, the *History of the Preceding Writing* was composed approximately in July 1776 and includes his *"Deposition Entrusted to Providence"* which we shall analyze later in this chapter.

In the *Dialogues*, the protagonists are Rousseau and *Le Français*, the latter being the spokesman for the calumnies against Jean-Jacques. The Frenchman had accused Rousseau of sensitivity on whatever affects his person, and indifference to what does not concern him. Rousseau admits that Jean-Jacques is endowed with a fairly high degree of physical sensitivity, particularly toward beauty in nature, and cites as an example his long daily walks during a complete spring season in order to hear the nightingale sing in the woods, in its natural surroundings. As far as moral sensitivity goes, he says that he knows no one who is as much affected by it as Jean-Jacques whose heart has a need to form attachments rather than be selective, and that trait has caused all the misfortunes of his life. Having then lost the sweetness of human society, solitude has become his lot, a sad lot, indeed, for man is made to be sociable and to crave for companionship. However, instead of becoming somber and taciturn, he still has a gay and serene expression, for he has found consolation and peace in nature and in God. Then, by "way of prayer,"[3] he cries out in the second dialogue:

> O Providence! o nature! treasure of the poor, resource of the unfortunate; he who feels, who knows Thy sacred laws and trusts them, he whose heart is at peace and whose body does not suffer, thanks to Thee, is not entirely prey to adversity. Despite all the plots of people, all the successes of the wicked, he cannot be completely miserable. Despoiled by cruel hands of all the good things in life, hope for a better future makes it up to him, imagination returns them to him at that very moment: happy imaginings replace real happiness; and—what am I saying? He alone is permanently happy, since material possessions can, at any time, be lost in a thousand ways to him who thinks he holds them for good: but nothing can take away the blessings that imagination bestows upon whoever knows how to enjoy them. He possesses

---

[3] Cf. Masson, *La Religion de Rousseau*, II, 232: "en guise de prière."

them without risk and without fear; neither fortune nor people could ever deprive him of them.[4]

Jean-Jacques has ever found inspiration, peace and consolation in nature. Religion, too, is, in his outlook, associated with feelings of natural beauty. When, therefore, he is disenchanted or disheartened by the adversity he encounters in society or by plots, real or imaginary, he returns to nature and in the midst of its beauty, such as a sunrise, he recaptures his calmness and his peace of mind. Then, he is spiritually elevated from nature to the God of nature to whom he prays. As Grimsley puts it: "Religion for Rousseau is an extension of nature, not its repudiation."[5] We are here far from the belief in a nature corrupted by man's original sin. Jean-Jacques views nature in positive terms only and this outlook is akin to deism or theism.

The closeness of the God of nature to His creation, nature, makes Rousseau, in our prayer, place them side by side and invoke them simultaneously ("O Providence, ô nature") as if they were one and the same, identical—almost a pantheistic concept. Masson's remarks also point in that direction: "The 'ways' of one seem to merge with the 'laws' of the other."[6] They "seem" to do so because of their proximity in Rousseau's mind but, close as they are, we cannot consider them, in fact, as identical, they do not coincide in Rousseau's conception. Let us then keep that distinction clear in our understanding of Rousseau.

---

[4]   Cf. *O.C.* I, 813–14: "O Providence! ô nature! trésor du pauvre, ressource de l'infortuné; celui qui sent, qui connaît vos saintes lois et s'y confie, celui dont le coeur est en paix et dont le corps ne souffre pas, grâce à vous n'est point tout entier en proie à l'adversité. Malgré tous les complots des homnes, tous les succès des méchants, il ne peut être absolument misérable. Dépouillé par des mains cruelles de tous les biens de cette vie, l'espérance l'en dédommage dans l'avenir, l'imagination les lui rend dans l'instant même: d'heureuses fictions lui tiennent lieu d'un bonheur réel; et que dis-je? Lui seul est solidement heureux, puisque les biens terrestres peuvent à chaque instant échapper en mille manières à celui qui croit les tenir: mais rien ne peut ôter ceux de l'imagination à quiconque sait en jouir. Il les possède sans risque et sans crainte; la fortune et les hommes ne sauraient l'en dépouiller."

[5]   Cf. Grimsley, *Religious Writings*, p. 139, note 4.

[6]   Cf. Masson, La *Religion de Rousseau*, II, 232: "Les 'voies' de l'un semblent se confondre avec les 'lois' de l'autre."

In his *Third Letter to Malesherbes* (1762), Jean-Jacques voices his ecstasy which, in turn, makes him, in his rapture, cry out to God words of adoration.[7] Here, he rather seeks refuge in nature as one runs to a loving, comforting mother to find solace and peace from adversity and real or imaginary plots which have plagued so often his life. The tone is not ecstatic but grave as he enumerates all the misfortunes befalling him. Nature is his island of retreat when the going is rough in society. Here, then, he finds something precious that money cannot buy, for material possessions are subject to fortune but spiritual gifts and the gift of a fertile imagination preserve man's happiness. One can also not be deprived of them since they are intangible and reside in the depth of our being. Jean-Jacques attached great weight to self-sufficiency, too, as a source of happiness. Here, it is with and through nature that he attains that goal.

B. Prayer to Providence as Arbiter of Justice

In his *History of the Preceding Writing*, Jean-Jacques relates how on Saturday, February 24, 1776, he made an attempt at depositing his *Dialogues* on which he had worked for four years, together with a prayer called "A Document Entrusted to Providence" on the high altar of the Cathedral of Notre Dame in Paris. He had thought that the manuscript would thus be handed over to the king and, this way, assure his vindication. Though he had made preliminary visits to the Church to familiarize himself with its layout, still, on that Saturday, to his surprise, he found the gates closed. Disappointed at first, he soon resorted to a rationalization: perhaps Providence wanted to prevent his manuscript "from falling into wrong hands at the king's court."

At that time, he heard of the presence of Condillac in the capital. Rousseau sees in this, too, the hand of Providence, and he entrusts the manuscript to Condillac, with the request that he give it to a younger, trustworthy person who would have to publish it at the end of the century. After the demise of Rousseau in 1778 and of Condillac in 1780, the promise was carried out by the latter's niece, Mme de Sainte-Foy, exactly on December 31, 1800.

---

[7] Cf .O.C. I, 1141. See above Chapter VI, section C.

Having second thoughts about Condillac, too, Jean-Jacques sees again the hand of Providence in the passing through Paris of a former neighbor of his in Wootton, England, Brooke-Boothby. He reasons that a foreigner may be more dependable because he is certainly not involved in plots against him. Rousseau manages to transcribe only the first dialogue and give it to Boothby who, it turned out, will prove truly dependable as he will publish it in May 1780, faithfully reproduced.

Still unsure that his self-justification will reach the public and anxious to break out of the circle in which he felt closed in by his enemies and their agents, Jean-Jacques writes a circular addressed to "Every Frenchman Who Still Loves Justice and Truth" and distributes it in the streets to people whose faces he likes in the hope of finding some to be of good faith. However, he registers no success in this project and he even ends up laughing himself at the response of people who said they did not qualify.

Finally, Jean-Jacques becomes more realistic and finds peace in the belief that somehow, regardless of what human beings may do, Heaven will have the final say and bring it about that his manuscript gets to its proper destination.

With this background showing us the importance Jean-Jacques attached to his self-justification in the Dialogues, let us read his prayer to God as the Supreme Arbiter of justice to whom alone he wanted to entrust the manuscript.

A Document Entrusted to Providence

God of justice and truth, Protector of the oppressed, receive this document placed on Thine altar and entrusted to Thy Providence by an unfortunate outsider who is alone, friendless and defenseless on this earth, insulted, mocked at, slandered, betrayed by a whole generation, on whom for the last fifteen years inflictions worse than death and indignities hitherto unknown among men have been showered, without his ever having been able to discover even their cause. I have been refused any explanation, I have no communication with my fellow-men, and can no longer expect from men, embittered by their own injustice, anything but injury, lies and betrayal. Eternal Providence, my only hope lies in Thee; take, I pray Thee, this document in Thy care and put it into young and faithful hands which will transmit it unadulterated to a better generation. May that generation, in lamenting my fate, learn what treatment was meted out to a guileless, inoffensive man who was opposed to injustice but endured it with patience, and who neither did evil nor returned it, nor ever wished it to be done. I know that no man has the right to expect a miracle, not even if he is the obscure and innocent victim of oppression. Since, one day, order will be re-established, it is enough to wait. Therefore, if my work has been wasted, if it is to be handed over to my enemies and, as seems inevitable, destroyed or defaced by them, I shall nevertheless place my trust in Thy taking action, although I do not know at what time and by what means; and after doing, as was proper, what I could to bring about a favorable outcome, I await the future with confidence, I put my faith in Thy justice and resign myself to Thy will.[8]

This prayer reflects Rousseau's deep distress caused by an exaggerated sense of being persecuted and maligned in his person and in his work, with no provision for self-defense and self-justification granted to him. Some critics have felt that Jean-Jacques had reached the edge of paranoia. Fortunately, his religious faith has provided both a counterweight to enable him not to lose balance and an address for final appeal as well as for unburdening himself. We are reminded of the psalmist's admission: "Unless Thy law (Torah, teaching) had been my delight, I should then have perished in mine

---

[8] Cf. *O.C.I*, 978–79: *Dépôt remis à la Providence.* "Protecteur des opprimés, Dieu de justice et de vérité, reçois ce dépôt qui remet sur ton autel et confie à ta providence un étranger infortuné, seul, sans appui, sans défenseur sur la terre, outragé, moqué, diffamé, trahi de toute une génération, chargé depuis quinze ans à l'envi de traitements pires que la mort et d'indignités inouïes jusqu'ici parmi les humains, sans avoir pu jamais en apprendre au moins la cause. Toute explication m'est refusée, toute communication m'est ôtée, je n'attends plus des hommes aigris par leur propre injustice qu'affronts, mensonges et trahisons. Providence éternelle, mon seul espoir est en toi; daigne prendre mon dépôt sous ta garde et le faire tomber en des mains jeunes et fidèles, qui le transmettent exempt de fraude à une meilleure génération; qu'elle apprenne en déplorant mon sort comment fut traité par celle-ci un homme sans fiel et sans fard, ennemi de l'injustice, mais patient à l'endurer, et qui jamais n'a fait, ni voulu, ni rendu de mal à personne. Nul n'a droit, je le sais, d'espérer un miracle, pas même l'innocence opprimée et méconnue. Puisque tout doit rentrer dans l'ordre un jour, il suffit d'attendre. Si donc mon travail est perdu, s'il doit être livré à mes ennemis et par eux détruit ou défiguré, comme cela paraît inévitable, je n'en compterai pas moins sur ton oeuvre, quoique j'en ignore l'heure et les moyens, et après avoir fait, comme je l'ai dû, mes efforts pour y concourir, j'attends avec confiance, je me repose sur ta justice, et me résigne à ta volonté."

affliction."[9] The plea of Rousseau is, indeed, addressed to the "God of justice and truth, Protector of the oppressed," as in the psalms which he chanted in his early youth in Geneva, a God who is man's confidant and who rights in His own time and way the wrongs committed in this His world. Jean-Jacques has become utterly despondent by his almost total isolation from human relationships ("I have no communication with my fellow-men") and, therefore, can only look upward, toward God, for assistance ("my only hope lies in Thee"). This prayer has also all the earmarks of a petitionary prayer. Under emotional stress, Rousseau has reverted to the mode of expression of his early beginnings. Yet, he is on guard not to cross certain limits that came to him from deism: for instance, not to ask, under any circumstances for a miracle. Apparent, too, is his selective reference to parts of the *Pater* used twice in this prayer ("it is enough to wait" and "I resign myself to Thy will") and expressing his submission to the Divine will. Equally notable is his explicit recourse to the principle of order in the universe, physical as well as moral ("since, one day, order will be re-established"). That principle of order, Grimsley emphasizes, "forms the basis of Rousseau's religious system."[10] It had been expressed before by the Vicar who said: "I see in the system of the world an order which remains unshaken."[11] Moreover, the Vicar retains an abiding belief in the emergence of that order in the next world if it be inoperative in this world: "Everything does not finish for us with life, everything returns to order at death."[12] Jean-Jacques refers in our prayer to this basic tenet of his *Weltanschauung* for it provides him with a measure of peace of mind which helps him bear the hardships and injustices of the present: "Since one day, order will be re-established, it is enough to wait." Though terms of renunciation and surrender alternate with terms of confidence and faith, nonetheless it is on a note of confidence and acceptance of the Divine will which, by definition, is just, that the prayer closes. Jean-Jacques has found and expressed in

---

[9]   Cf. Psalms, cxix.92.

[10] Cf. Grimsley, *Religious Writings*, p. 146, note 2.

[11] Cf. *Profession de foi*, O.C. IV, 588: "je vois dans le système du monde un ordre qui ne se dément pas."

[12] Ibid., p. 590: "Tout ne finit pas pour nous avec la vie, tout rentre dans l'ordre à la mort."

this prayer some balance between despair and hope because of his religious beliefs. As he had written in his 1756 letter to Voltaire, nothing can make him doubt for a moment the immortality of the soul and the existence of a benevolent Providence.

CHAPTER XIII

Conclusion

The student of eighteenth-century French literature is impressed by
the galaxy of original writers who dealt mainly with two fundamental
elements of the personal and social fabric: religion and politics.
Nothing was spared by the new inquiry which, in the name of
enlightenment, reason and natural religion, submitted everything to a
sharp, merciless reappraisal. Past conceptions were scrutinized and
evaluated—and found wanting. Most outstanding writers would see
their role as that of clearing the ground from accepted, superannuated
notions not conforming with what they believed rational thinking
demanded, and proposing new values in their stead. In particular,
religion (i.e. Christianity for which Bossuet had feared the
indiscriminate application of Cartesian rationalism and, for tactical
reasons, the Hebrew Scriptures too) was consequently subjected to
unceasing, persistent attacks. The old world was crumbling and what
appeared as an indicator of the world to come was so radical that it
frightened even a *philosophe* like Voltaire who also wanted to destroy
the old "superstitions" but refused to replace them by the other
extreme—a materialistic atheism. Yet, Voltaire's deism was too
abstract, too rationalistic, too cold, to stem the tide. It was too much a
construction of the human mind, regarding God as a Divine
Architect, a Divine Watchmaker or a Cosmic Policeman rather than a
God who relates to people. Then, from the very midst of the
philosophes, there arose Jean-Jacques Rousseau who knew the
intellectual climate of the time and yet, acting against the trend of the
century, promulgated early in his career a positive outlook on
religion, morality and prayer. To be sure, he adopted the deism of the
day which, it should be added, was by no means uniform. Soon,
however, he went his own way, leaving his erstwhile "philosophic"
friends behind, blazing a new trail and sounding a new call to

conscience, morality, justice and rehabilitation of the religious sentiment and "the rights of the heart" by which one can arrive at belief in God. It was he, Jean-Jacques, as he was affectionately called in Europe, who took it upon himself to challenge the great of his day. Mario Einaudi brings us H.F. Amiel's summary of Rousseau's role in a striking, schematic fashion: "He [Rousseau] was for God against d'Holbach, he was for Providence against Voltaire, he found a soul in man against La Mettrie, he was for moral freedom against Diderot, for disinterested virtues against Helvétius, for spontaneity against Condillac, for the rights of the heart against Maupertuis, against the communism of Morelly, against the absolutism of Hobbes."[1] Then Einaudi adds: "Indeed, Rousseau's protest is directed against 'the very essence of contemporary society.'[2] Against the prevailing corruption, he wants to protect his freedom and independence. Against greed and wealth, he wants to be poor. Against unbelief and skepticism, he is anxious to reaffirm a belief in God and a faith which his communion with the *encyclopédistes*, 'far from weakening, had only strengthened!'"[3] In his letter to the Archbishop of Paris, M. de Beaumont, Jean-Jacques described himself as "the defender of the cause of God."[4] In a century so dominated by gifted, vocal critics of traditionalism, he does stand out as an influential, eloquent exception and corrector who, as skilled in the use of the literary tool as his opponents and detractors, can point in a different direction, toward positive values in religion and in man's existential need to pray. It is not in vain that many contemporaries of his, both clergymen and laymen, turned to him with their religious doubts, for he was able to provide them with positive guidance strengthening their basic beliefs.

It has been said that the greatness of man resides in his ability to stand before God and to address himself to God. The frequent resorting to prayer in those of Rousseau's writings that lend themselves to it is indicative of that quality of greatness in Jean-Jacques who be-

---

[1] Mario Einaudi, *The Early Rousseau* (Ithica, N.Y.: Cornell University Press, 1967), pp. 55–56, quoting H.F. Amiel, *Caractéristique générale de Rousseau*, pp. 44–45.

[2] Ibid., p. 56, quoting Jean Starobinsky, *Jean-Jacques Rousseau, la transparence et l'obstacle*, p. 44.

[3] Ibid., p. 56, quoting *Les Confessions*, Book 8, O.C. I, 392.

[4] Cf. *Lettre à M. de Beaumont*, O.C. IV, 931: "le défenseur de la cause de Dieu."

lieved that man lives in an ever-present companionship with God and is the constant object of God's gaze. It is in the open air, in the surroundings of the beauty of nature, that Rousseau personally can best pray, that Rousseau is most inspired to pray. The earliest known prayers by Jean-Jacques are those which he wrote at Les Charmettes. They contain mostly traditional elements, such as humility, unworthiness, petition, repentance, in its fullest sense leading to new resolutions for the future, mention of human misery, even belief in *creatio ex nihilo* and, of course, intercalated between two paragraphs, the complete, official *Pater* prayer. An anticipatory deistic element, such as direct communication with God, makes its appearance here. In a second phase, we find side by side with these traditional elements, also elements of deism or natural religion: the concept of nature as source of revelation of God ("King of nature") and of inspiration of man to reach God with the corollary that nature is good; the engraving of Divine law in the human heart; Divine mercy being at least equal to his majesty; superiority of deeds over creed. Concomitantly, we find no reference to Jesus and the cardinal Christian dogmas, such as original sin, the concept of the Trinity, the sacraments, the saints. This absence, it should be noted, will be constant throughout Rousseau's life and will be maintained consistently in all his prayers, even those composed in a state of high emotion. In a third phase, theistic elements appear. They include many deistic components which are common to both deism and theism but with the addition of specifically theistic principles, such as helief in a personal God and in a personal Providence symbolized by the Divine gaze.

The two earliest prayers of Jean-Jacques presage the direction of his future prayers. The traditional elements in those two prayers will be reduced in the later ones. Even the official *Pater* prayer will emerge in one of its requests, mainly submissiveness to the will of God ("Thy will be done"). Deistic elements will be widened to include conscience, for instance, as the highest rule in man, while the distance between man and God—a transcendental God—will be underscored, with prayers usually expressing adoration, homage, contemplation, thanksgiving. At the extreme, Rousseau will be so filled with enthusiasm (literal meaning in Greek: God in me) that he will remain almost speechless, repeatedly uttering only an exclamation to God "Oh great

Being" or in ecstasy saying only "O!" At other times, adoration will reach its ultimate expression in utter silence or in silent wonder—a prayer without words, an inner act of prayer by the heart and not a prayer verbalized by the lips. As Rousseau's career unfolds, theistic elements will become affirmed and emphasized above all in situations of stress and high emotional upsurge, whether it be Julie, after her marriage, soliciting Divine help to strengthen her resolution or Jean-Jacques entrusting a document to God whom he considers a confidant as well as the arbiter of justice and to whom he turns to right the wrongs committed against him. Theistic prayer emphasizes God's nearness, God's immanence, and the appeal is a direct appeal to a personal Providence as opposed to the impersonal Providence of deism. While the beliefs in the immortality of the soul and in the hereafter are present in traditional, deistic and theistic approaches to religion, they occupy an especially important position in Rousseau's thought because they constitute for him the indispensable compensation of a just God for all his sufferings in this world.

The importance attached to prayer by Rousseau is also demonstrated by the fact that we find in his writings long discussions on the function, the definition and the many facets of prayer, particularly petitionary prayer. We have attempted to show in our critique that, from a logical and certainly a religious viewpoint, the dividing line between prayers of praise and homage and petitionary prayer is arbitrary, and also that prayer in general has meaning only in a theistic frame of reference which, coincidentally, is also Rousseau's practice if not always his theoretical position (as evidenced by Saint-Preux and the Vicar both rejecting for themselves petitionary prayer). Rousseau's prayer is also individual and not social prayer. He requires for it sincerity, depth of emotion and inner identification with what is being expressed. Whether it be Julie, Saint-Preux or the Vicar who act as his representatives, or Jean-Jacques speaking in his self-defense about prayer in his letter to M. de Beaumont or in his letter to God which he wanted to place on the altar of a Church, Rousseau everywhere manifests a serious attitude toward prayer. Prayer surges up in many parts of his writings, unexpectedly, even though it is organically linked to the text. This amply illustrates how natural a place prayer occupied in his outlook. And it is not a crutch, such as religion itself has at times been described to be by non-religionists. It is rather the spontaneous outpouring of the human heart to its Creator. For to Rousseau, let us not forget, man lives constantly under the watchful eye of God. Viewed from this perspective, life becomes a serious matter and prayer an important act in which we take heed of the Divine presence.[5] In philosophic terms, God's transcendence alone is insufficient to Jean-Jacques. He needs immanence as well in order to be able to relate to God. Deity is a living God to him and not a construct of the human mind. Pomeau characterizes Rousseau's conception of God as the "Physician of his soul."[6] This concept of a living God exists in all of Rousseau's prayers side by side with essentials of deism, such as a preference for limitation of prayer to adoration and homage and the like and the absence of any Christological references. Only once, in a quasi-prayer, as we have shown, does he mention Jesus and there too, it is not for direct invocation. However, he follows his deistic concepts as to what prayers are admissible only as long as cool reason controls his writing. When his emotion dominates, the nature of his prayers quickly shifts from what detached deism would require and abounds in expressions indicating deeply-felt theism. Rousseau's rapport with God becomes then very personal, bilateral, a dialogue, a desire for fellowship with God.

Rousseau's theism, as we have noted, approximates remarkably closely the universal religion of Noahism with its seven commandments. Noahism is "as old as creation," which is also a criterion of natural religion, and is based on God's relationship with Noah at the beginning of the Biblical book of Genesis. The Sages of the Talmud[7] constantly emphasize that, according to Judaism, the "seven commandments of Noah's descendants" constitute the binding law of mankind. Of course, in Jewish tradition Noahism, too, is a revealed religion. However, in Jewish religious thought, singularly gifted peo-

---

[5]   Cf. Burgelin, *La Philosophie de l'existence de J.-J. Rousseau*, p. 460.

[6]   Cf. Pomeau, *La Religion de Voltaire*, p. 420.

[7]   In his *Letter to M. de Beaumont*, *O.C.* IV, 1974, Rousseau alludes to Talmud and Mishnah in this order, though the Mishnah (and not Misnah) precedes chronologically and is also included in the Talmud. To put it graphically: Mishnah plus its amplification called Gemara equal Talmud or the Oral Law of Judaism. To our knowledge, Rousseau does not seem to show acquaintanceship with any of its teachings though he uses the terms as analogy in this letter.

ple, searching honestly and with their passions and prejudices silenced, can discover truths that approximate revealed teachings. The sensitive, introspective and truth-obsessed Jean-Jacques thus reached through his own search and thinking a form of religion which is generally called theism but which, we find, coincides with the Jewish revealed conception of what the universal religion of the world ought to be. Toward the end of his books on Rousseau's religion, the erudite Masson, to our surprise, finds in Jean-Jacques not only echoes of the Psalmist but also of Isaiah and Jeremiah "whom he has loved so much." His only reservation is that, unlike "the prophets of Israel, he has not kept the sense of repentance, and of remorse which regenerates, and of expiation which absolves."[8]

Contemporary writers have been in accord about Rousseau's impact on modern life. A proponent of Jean-Jacques, Einaudi, writes thus: "Today Rousseau is increasingly seen as the most influential thinker of the eighteenth century. His views on man and society, on private and public life, on economics and government, seem astonishingly relevant to twentieth-century problems. He is, therefore, being read now with a care and a thoroughness he did not always get in his own time and for many years afterward. Perhaps only in the last two generations has Rousseau's thought, in all its extraordinary complexity, begun to be fully understood."[9] A modern opponent of Rousseau, the novelist François Mauriac, also admits fascination with Jean-Jacques today and adds: ". . . a literary work must have strong vitality if, a century and a half later [after it was written], we do not cease defending ourselves against it—and with what vehemence!"[10]

To his own century, weary of excessive rationalism, Jean-Jacques showed that the needs of the mind must go hand in hand with the needs of the heart. To him rightfully belongs the glory of rediscovery of the roots of man's moral and spiritual existence and, with it, the language of faith—prayer, for his time and ours as well.

---

[8] Cf. Masson, *La Religion de Rousseau*, III, 354.

[9] Cf .Einaudi, preface, p. v.

[10] Cf. Mauriac, p. 93.

Bibliography

Books of the Bible are not listed in this bibliography unless reference is made to a
particular edition.

Primary Sources

Rousseau, Jean-Jacques. *Correspondance générale de Jean-Jacques Rousseau.* Colationnée
par Théophile Dufour. Paris: Librairie Armand Colin, 1924–1934.
———. *Oeuvres complèetes.* Ed. Bernard Gagnebin and Marcel Raymond. Bibliothèque
de la Pléiade. Paris: Gallimard.
Vol. I (1959). *Les Confessions; Rousseau juqe de Jean-Jacques—Dialogues; Les Rêveries
du promeneur solitaire; Fragments autobiographiques et documents biographiques;
Lettres à Malesherbes; Notes et variantes.*
Vol. II (1961). *Julie ou La Nouvelle Héloïse; Notices bibliographiques; Notes et
variantes.*
Vol. III (1964). *Discours sur les sciences et les arts; Lettres écrites de la montagne; Du
Contrat social; Notes et variantes; Fragments politiques.*
Vol. IV (1969). *Emile ou De L'Education; La Profession de foi du vicaire savoyard;
Lettre à Christophe de Beaumont; . Fragments sur Dieu et sur la révélation (Prières);
Lettre à Voltaire sur la Providence; Lettre à Franquières; Notes et variantes.*

Secondary Sources

Albo, Joseph. *Sefer Ha'ikkarim—Book of Principles.* Trans. Isaac Husik. Philadelphia:
Jewish Publication Society, 1930. V-01. IV.
Baudelaire, Charles. *Intimate Journals.* London: Blackamore Press; New York: Random
House, 1930.
Berkovits, Eliezer. *Studies in Torah Judaism—Prayer.* New York: Yeshiva University,
1962.
Burgelin, Pierre. *Jean-Jacques Rousseau et la religion de Genève.* Genève: Editions Labor
et Fides, 1962; Paris: Diffusion en France, Librairie Protestante.
———. *La Philosophie de l'existence de Jean-Jacques Rousseau.* Paris: Presses
universitaires de France, 1952.

Crocker, Lester J. "Confessions de Jean-Jacques Rousseau," *Explication de texte*. Ed. Jean Sareil. Vol. I, 2nd ed. Englewood Cliffs, N.J.: Prentice Hall, 1970.

De Feller, Abbé F.X. *Catéchisme philosophique ou Recueil d'observations propres à défendre la religion chrétienne contre ses ennemis*. Lyon: Périsse frères; Paris: Au dépôt de la librairie de Périsse frères, 1830. Vol. III.

Dufour, Théophile. *Annales de la société Jean-Jacques Rousseau*. Genève: A. Jullien. Vol. I (1905) and Vol. XXXV (1959/62).

Einaudi, Mario. *The Early Rousseau*. Ithaca, N.Y.: Cornell University Press, 1967.

Encyclopedia of Religion and Ethics. G.C., J[oyce] and C.F. D'Arcy. Vol. IV (1928) and Vol. X (1928).

Fellows, Otis E. and Norman L. Torrey. *The Age of. Enlightenment*. New York: Appleton-Century-Crofts, 1942.

Gay, Peter. *Deism: An Anthology*. Princeton, N.J.: Van Nostrand, 1968.

Gouhier, Henri. *Les Méditations philosophiques de Jean-Jacques Rousseau*. Paris: Librairie philosophique J. Vrin, 1970.

Green, F.C. *Jean-Jacques Rousseau—A Critical Study of His Life and Writings*. Cambridge: University Press, 1955.

Grimsley, Ronald. *Jean-Jacques Rousseau—Religious Writings*. Oxford: Clarendon Press, 1970.

Grimsley, Ronald. *Rousseau and the Religious Quest*. Oxford: Clarendon Press, 1968.

Guéhenno, Jean. *Jean-Jacques Rousseau*. Trans. John and Doreen Weightman. London: Routledge and Kegan Paul; New York: Columbia University Press, 1966.

Guyot, Charly. *De Rousseau à Marcel Proust*. Neuchâtel: Editions Ides et Calendes, 1968.

Havens, George R. *The Age of Ideas*. New York: Free Press, 1966.

Hendel, Charles W. *Jean-Jacques Rousseau Moralist*. Library of Liberal Arts. Indianapolis, New York: Bobbs-Merrill, 1934.

Hertz, Joseph H. *A Book of Jewish Thoughts*. New York: Bloch Publishing Co., 1953.

———. *The Authorized Daily Prayer Book*. Revised ed. New York: Bloch Publishing Co., 1948.

Höffding, Harald. *Jean-Jacques Rousseau and his Philosophy*. Trans. from second Danish edition by William Richards and Leo E. Saidla. New Haven: Yale University Press, 1930.

Hugo, Victor. *La Légende des siècles*. Paris: Bibliothèque de la Pléiade, 1950.

Kant, Immanuel. Religion Within the Limits of Reason Alone. Trans. with introduction and notes by Theodore M. Greene and Hoyt H. Hudson. First published La Salle, Illinois: Open Court Publishing Company, 1934, reprinted New York: Harper and Brothers, 1960.

Maimonides, Moses. *Mishneh Torah*. (Code of Jewish law.)

———. *The Guide of the Perplexed*. Trans. and annotated by M. Friedlander. New York: Hebrew Publishing Company, n.d.

Masson, Pierre-Maurice. *La Religion de Jean-Jacques Rousseau*. 2nd ed. Paris: Librairie Hachette, 1916.

———. *La Profession de foi du vicaire savoyard*. Introduction et commentaire. Fribourg:

Librairie de l'universit, 1914.

Mauriac, François. *Trois Grands Hommes devant Dieu*. Paris: Editions du Capitole, 1930.

Mauzi, Robert. "La Conversion de Julie dans La Nouvelle Héloïse" in *Annales de la Société Jean-Jacques Rousseau*. Genève: Chez ,4. Jullien, 1959/62, Vol. XXXV.

Midrash Rabbah on Exodus. Tel Aviv: A. Halevy, 1959.

Midrash Tehillim (Midrash on the Psalms). Ed. Solomon Buber.

Mishnah. *Yaddayim*.

Morais, Herbert M. *Deism in Eighteenth-Century America*, issued as Columbia University dissertation in 1934 and printed in New York: Russell and Russell, 1960.

Mornet, Daniel. *"La Nouvelle Héloïse" de Jean-Jacques Rousseau*. Etude et analyse. Paris: Editions Mellottée, 1929.

Munk, Elie. *The World of Prayer*. New York: Philipp Feldheim, 1963. Vol. II.

New Catholic Encyclopedia. R.Z. L[auer], 1967. Vol. IV.

New Encyclopaedia Britannica—Macropaedia. A [dalbert] G. Ha[mman], Vol. XIV (1974). F[rank] E[dward] M[anuel], Vol. V (1974).

Pallière, Aimé. *The Unknown Sanctuary*. Trans. Louise Waterman Wise. New York: Bloch Publishing Co., 1928.

Pomeau, René. *La Religion de Voltaire*. Paris: Nizet, 1956.

———. *Julie ou La Nouvelle Héloïse*. Introduction. Paris: Garnier, 1960.

Psalms. Hebrew Text, English Translation and Commentary. Ed. A. Cohen. Hindhead, Surrey: The Soncino Press,

Ramban (Nachmanides). *Commentary on the Torah*. Book of Genesis. Trans. and annotation Charles B. Chavel. New York: Shilo Publishing House, 1971.

Richard, François and Pierre. *"Emile ou De L'Education" de J.-J. Rousseau*. Paris: Garnier, 1951.

Rolland, Romain. *French Thought in the Eighteenth Century*. New York: David McKay, 1953.

Schinz, Albert. *La Pensée religieuse de Rousseau et ses récents interprètes*. Paris: Alcan, 1927.

Schinz, Albert. *Vie et oeuvres de Jean-Jacques Rousseau*. Boston, New York, Chicago: D.C. Heeth, 1921.

Talmud. Tractates of *Berakhoth, Shabbat, Haggigah, Sanhedrin, Taanith, Avoth d'Rabbi Nathan*.

Torrey, Norman L. *Voltaire and the English Deists*. Hamden, Conn.: Archon Books, 1967.

———. *The Spirit of Voltaire*. New York: Russell and Russell, 1938. Reissued 1968.

Van Tieghem, Philippe. *"La Nouvelle Héloïse" de Jacques Rousseau*. Paris: Nizet, 1956.

Vartanian, Ararn. "From Deist to Atheist: Diderot's Philosophical Orientation, 1746–1749." In *Diderot Studies*, ed. Otis E. Fellows and Norman L. Torrey. Syracuse, N.Y.: Syracuse University Press, 1949. Vol. I.

Voltaire. *Dictionnaire philosophique*. Paris: Classiques Garnier, 1961. Trans. Peter Gay. *Philosophical Dictionary*. New York: Basic Books, 1962. Vol. II.